THE LAW OF CONFIDENTIALITY

The last twenty years have seen rapid development of the equitable action for breach of confidence. The Spycatcher saga of the late 1980s led to the restatement of the fundamental principles. There was increasing concern about press intrusion, and the need to protect privacy rights guaranteed by Article 8 of the European Convention in the wake of the Human Rights Act 1998. Against that background, a number of high-profile cases—such as *Campbell v MGN Ltd* (2004)—explored how common law principles laid down in the nineteenth century might be adapted to twenty-first century conditions. How far will the law go in protecting privacy? Meanwhile, in the 'information age', the law has had to grapple—for instance in *Douglas v Hello! Ltd* (2007)—with how best to protect the commercially valuable information and when it should assist those who wish to exploit it.

The result has been rapid development of the law in many diverse areas. *The Law of Confidentiality: A Restatement* goes behind the mass of cases to tease out the fundamental principles underlying the modern law. It examines the important questions of substance: the circumstances in which information is protected by law, and how it responds to conflicting public interests. It also looks at the important practical questions of procedure and remedies. It aims to be useful to those looking for a guide to the main principles and controversies in the field, and also to the practising lawyer looking for a clear statement of the basic principles.

The Law of Confidentiality
A Restatement

Paul Stanley

• HART •
OXFORD • LONDON • NEW YORK • NEW DELHI • SYDNEY

HART PUBLISHING
Bloomsbury Publishing Plc
Kemp House, Chawley Park, Cumnor Hill, Oxford, OX2 9PH, UK

HART PUBLISHING, the Hart/Stag logo, BLOOMSBURY and the Diana logo are trademarks of Bloomsbury Publishing Plc
First published in Great Britain 2008

First published in hardback, 2008

A catalogue record for this book is available from the British Library.

ISBN: 978-1-84113-811-4

Typeset by Hope Services, Abingdon

Preface

One fascination of the common law of confidentiality is that so many specialists bring their particular concerns and characteristic techniques to bear upon it. They also approach it wearing their particular blinkers. Thus commercial lawyers bring an intense focus on the express terms and commercial practicalities of particular economic relationships. But in doing so they sometimes give too little attention to the *public* interests at stake, and seek the comfortable certainty of over-rigid rules. Family lawyers contribute a sharp appreciation for the multiplicity and complexity of human interests, the unique importance of each situation. But in doing so they sometimes brush aside technical and formal concern with the structure of the law, and reach (perhaps too quickly?) for a discretionary sword with which to cut Gordian knots. Intellectual property lawyers understand better than anyone how crucial intangible rights can be for business, and many of the techniques by which they can be most soundly protected and vindicated. But they may be too swift to treat all rights as if they were intellectual *property* rights. Similar points, both positive and negative, can be made about the other specialists whose contribution has been so great—equity lawyers, media and defamation specialists, human rights lawyers. Each brings a particular set of intellectual tools, designed to deal with a distinctive set of problems.

Above all, now, the law of confidentiality needs systematic treatment, so that the best insights offered by so many different approaches are applied consistently, and the less fruitful or counter-productive ones are eliminated or controlled. Sterling work has been done by a number of authors in this direction: by Francis Gurry, Robert Dean, Sir Roger Toulson and Charles Phipps in particular, but by no means only by them. Nobody curious about confidentiality law could manage without them. This book, I hope, takes a slightly different approach. My aim has been to be less discursive, even at the risk of being dogmatic in stating what I understand to be the core principles. Whatever its disadvantages (apart from being unfashionable), the form of pseudo-code and commentary does at least help to expose the structure of the law, and forces an author to take a stand. My aim has been to provide a brief and systematic exposition of core principles, with a focus which is practical without being entirely uncritical, which may help organise thinking and guide research into the more detailed specialist works.

The restatement in §§ 1 to 26 sets out the common law as I understand it to be on 8 November 2007. This left a few loose ends. In particular, some negative statements ('detriment is not required', 'information is not property', 'breach of confidence does not give rise to a constructive trust') hardly belonged in the main sections, but do deserve some discussion. These are confined to appendices.

Many people have helped me while I was writing this book. Claire Blanchard, Martin Griffiths, Lord Neuberger, Luan Ong, Sue Prevezer, Amy Sander, John Stanley and Emily Wood all helped in various ways, reading parts of the text or discussing particular points of difficulty. Thomas Ford provided valuable research assistance and improved the text in many ways. My children, Benedict and Zachary, and my partner Daniel Slater (who also read much of the manuscript) provided support and encouragement. I am grateful to all of them.

Paul Stanley
Lincoln's Inn Fields
8 November 2007

Contents

Table of Cases

Table of Statutes and Statutory Instruments

Abbreviations

Dean: R Dean, *The Law of Trade Secrets and Personal Secrets,* 2nd edn (Pyrmont, 2002)

Gurry: F Gurry, *Breach of Confidence* (Oxford, 1984)

Meagher; Gummow & Lehane: Meagher; Heydon and Leeming, *Meagher, Gummow and Lehane's Equity: Doctrines and Remedies*; 4th edn (Chatswood NSW, 2002)

Toulson & Phipps: R G Toulson and C M Phipps, *Confidentiality,* 2nd ed (London, 2006)

Tugendhat & Christie: M Tugendhat and I Christie, *The Law of Privacy and the Media* (Oxford, 2002)

Part I

The Duty of Confidence

§ 1

The Basic Principle

Information is protected as confidential where the claimant has a reasonable expectation of confidentiality or privacy, and the defendant has agreed to keep the information confidential or has notice of its confidentiality.

INTRODUCTION

IT WAS LONG ago established that equity will enforce obligations between persons who are or have been in a relationship of 'confidence' with each other. Thus if, within the framework of a confidential relationship, *A* communicated information to *B* on terms that *B* would keep the information secret, equity would intervene to require *B* to comply with his obligations. In effect, whether or not the relationship was strictly one of contract in the legal sense, equity enforced obligations which were consensually assumed. (Many cases of confidentiality are still of this sort, in that they rest on an underlying consensual *agreement* between the parties that *B* will keep something secret.)

That dealt with the position as between *A* and *B*. But what if, perhaps in breach of his obligations, *B* communicated the information to a third person, *C*? In strict terms, *C* would never have promised *A* to keep the information secret. But equity was not deterred: provided *C* knew that the information was something that *B* had agreed to keep confidential, equity would impose a similar obligation upon C. This development occurred by the middle of the nineteenth century in *Prince Albert v Strange*.[1] It remained the essential basis of the equitable action for breach of confidence until the last decade of the twentieth century—that information having the 'necessary quality of confidence' had been 'imparted in circumstances importing an obligation of confidence',[2] of which the defendant was aware, or was to be taken as having been aware. The

[1] (1849) 1 Mac & G 25.

[2] *Coco v A N Clark (Engineers) Ltd* [1969] RPC 41, 47 (Megarry J).

information was not property in the strict sense, but equity would 'restrain its transmission to another if in breach of some confidential relationship'.[3]

The focus on the 'confidential relationship', however, remained a limiting factor.[4] In particular, if *C* acquired information *directly* from or about *A*, but without anything that could be regarded as a confidential relationship between *A* and *C*, the case was difficult to accommodate within the traditional approach.[5] Thus potentially hard cases included those where C obtained the information by eavesdropping or intrusion,[6] and those where *C* obtained the information by chance: the confidential diary that floated out of an open window.

In the *Spycatcher* case,[7] Lord Goff took the analysis a stage further,[8] by removing the need for some pre-existing 'confidential relationship':

> I start with the broad general principle . . . that a duty of confidence arises when confidential information comes to the knowledge of a person (the confidant) in circumstances where he has notice, or is held to have agreed, that the information is confidential, with the effect that it would be just in all the circumstances that he should be precluded from disclosing the information to others.[9]

As Lord Goff explained:

> I have expressed the circumstances in which the duty arises in broad terms, not merely to embrace those cases where a third party receives information from a person who is under a duty of confidence in respect of it, knowing that it has been disclosed by that person to him in breach of his duty of confidence, but also to include certain situations . . . where an obviously confidential document is wafted by an electric fan out of a window into a crowded street, or where an obviously confidential document, such as a private diary, is dropped in a public place, and is then picked up by a passer-by. I also have in mind the situations where secrets of importance to national security come into the possession of members of the public.[10]

Freed of the imperative requirement to identify a 'confidential relationship', the law was readily able to find a duty of confidence when the information was extracted not by agreement, but unwillingly or even without the claimant's consent. By 1994, Laws J was able to state confidently:

[3] *Boardman v Phipps* [1967] 2 AC 46 (HL), 128 (Lord Upjohn). See also *Seager v Copydex Ltd* [1967] 1 WLR 923 (CA), 961 (Lord Denning MR) referring to the 'broad principle of equity that he who has received information in confidence shall not take unfair advantage of it.'

[4] See, eg, *Malone v Metropolitan Police Commissioner* [1979] Ch 344, 376 (Megarry V-C). As Meagher, Gummow & Lehane point out, at para 41–045, the Vice-Chancellor had been 'led into a cul-de-sac' by a search for consensual dealing between claimant and defendant.

[5] Though some work could be done by stretching the categories of 'confidential' relationships, as in *Argyll v Argyll* [1967] Ch 302 and *Stephens v Avery* [1988] Ch 449.

[6] As, for instance, in the timorous decision in *Kaye v Robertson* [1991] FSR 62 (CA).

[7] *Attorney-General v Guardian Newspapers* (*No 2*) [1990] 1 AC 109 (HL).

[8] This was not an unexpected development. It was prefigured in, for instance, *Franklin v Giddins* [1978] Qd R 72 (Dunn J).

[9] [1990] 1 AC 109, 281.

[10] *Ibid.*

> If someone with a telephoto lens were to take from a distance and with no authority a picture of another engaged in some private act, his subsequent disclosure of the photograph would . . . as surely amount to a breach of confidence as if he had found or stolen a letter or diary in which the act was recounted and proceeded to publish it.[11]

That quotation reflects a second trend in the case law, during the last quarter of the twentieth century or so: the courts' increased willingness to protect personal as well as commercial secrets. Until the late 1970s, most (though not all) cases were concerned with the protection of confidence in a commercial context—with trade or business secrets. Increasingly, however, cases came before the courts where confidentiality was deployed to protect non-commercial secrets.[12] It came to be accepted, though with some reservations,[13] that the law of confidence could be used to protect secrets such as sexual matters.[14] These developments were already taking place before the Human Rights Act 1998—but the need to find a place in English law for protections which would satisfy the requirements of Article 8 of the European Convention on Human Rights gave them added force. Combined with the loosening of any requirement to establish a consensual relationship of confidence, the effect of these developments was that 'the law would protect what might reasonably be called a right of privacy, although the name accorded to the cause of action would be breach of confidence.'[15]

THE MODERN POSITION

Since *Spycatcher*, then, it has been clear that protection does not depend upon the existence of any confidential relationship, as such—though there often will be one. That leaves open the question: What standard is to be applied?

Lord Goff's *Spycatcher* formulation referred simply to 'confidential information'. In later cases, the courts grappled more closely with what makes information 'confidential'. A generally applicable standard was suggested in *Campbell v MGN Ltd*.[16] Lord Nicholls pointed out that the action for breach of confidence had 'firmly shaken off the limiting constraint of the need for an initial confidential relationship'.[17] English law would now protect not only commercially confidential information, or information imparted 'in confidence', but also information about an individual's private life. He continued:

[11] *Hellewell v Chief Constable of Derbyshire* [1995] 1 WLR 804, 807.

[12] The distinction is not completely clear, however. Many of the cases concerning 'personal' privacy relate to celebrities, whose 'image' is itself valuable, and commercially exploited.

[13] See, *eg*, the decision of Garland J in *M v McKenzie* (18 Jan 1988), unreported, described in *Stephens v Avery* [1988] Ch 449, 456.

[14] See, in particular, *Argyll v Argyll* [1967] Ch 302; *Khashoggi v Smith* (1980) 124 SJ 149 (CA); *Stephens v Avery* [1988] Ch 449.

[15] *Hellewell v Chief Constable of Derbyshire* [1995] 1 WLR 804, 807 (Laws J).

[16] [2004] UKHL 22, [2004] 2 AC 457.

[17] *Ibid*, [14].

> Essentially the touchstone of private life is whether in respect of the disclosed facts the person in question had a reasonable expectation of privacy.[18]

Lord Hope referred to the defendant being in a:

> situation where he knows or ought to know that the other person can reasonably expect his privacy to be protected.[19]

The 'reasonable expectations' test has attracted academic approval[20] and has since been used by the Court of Appeal in a number of subsequent cases: *Douglas v Hello! Ltd (No 3)*,[21] the *Royal Diaries* case,[22] and *Lord Browne of Madingley v Associated Newspapers*.[23] There is some variation in the terminology used. Although it is clear that English law protects personal privacy and other forms of confidentiality using the same 'cause of action' (the historic action for breach of confidence) and not a distinct 'privacy tort',[24] it is recognised that some cases (especially those of commercially confidential information and those which feature a traditional 'confidential relationship') are more appropriately described using the language of 'confidence' and 'confidentiality', and others more aptly make use of the terminology of 'privacy'.[25]

Moreover, although we are dealing here with a single tort or equitable wrong, the context can matter. Cases asserting an 'old-fashioned breach of confidence'[26] may well be best addressed by considering established authority.[27] Cases raising issues of personal privacy which might engage Article 8 of the Convention will require special focus on the case law of the European Court of Human Rights concerning that article. There must, in short, be some flexibility in recognition of the different interests and circumstances that individual cases may raise. Nevertheless, the general test set out in § 1 seems broad enough to encompass both the old-fashioned and the new-fangled.[28]

[18] [2004] UKHL 22, [2004] 2 AC 457, [21].

[19] [2004] UKHL 22, [2004] 2 AC 457, [85], adopting a statement of Lord Woolf CJ in *A v B plc* [2002] EWCA Civ 337, [2003] QB 195, [11]. Baroness Hale adopted the same test: [2004] UKHL 22, [2004] 2 AC 457, [134].

[20] N A Moreham, 'Privacy in the Common Law: A Doctrinal and Theoretical Analysis' (2005) 121 *LQR* 628, 630–36, 644–45.

[21] [2005] EWCA Civ 595, [2006] QB 125, [100].

[22] *HRH Prince of Wales* v *Associated Newspapers Ltd* [2006] EWCA Civ 1776, [2007] 3 WLR 222, [34].

[23] [2007] EWCA Civ 295, [2007] 3 WLR 289.

[24] *Wainwright v Home Office* [2003] UKHL 53, [2004] 2 AC 406.

[25] See, in particular, *McKennitt v Ash* [2006] EWCA Civ 1714, [2007] 3 WLR 194, [8].

[26] *Ibid*.

[27] For instance, cases of commercial confidentiality may well be approached by reference to the classic test propounded by Megarry J in *Coco v A N Clark (Engineers) Ltd* [1969] RPC 41, 47, as happened in *Douglas v Hello! Ltd (No 3)* in the House of Lords: [2007] UKHL 21, [2007] 2 WLR 920

[28] The controversial question whether it would be better to recognise separate wrongs of breach of confidence and interference with privacy is addressed in Appendix C.

§ 2

Reasonable Expectation of Confidentiality

In deciding whether a claimant has a reasonable expectation of confidentiality, all the circumstances of the case are considered, but particular attention is paid to—

(*a*) any relationship between the claimant and a confidant within which the information was acquired;
(*b*) how far access to the information was limited to a restricted group of people;
(*c*) the nature of the information, and in particular its subject-matter, form and sensitivity for the claimant;
(*d*) whether the information has been communicated for a specific purpose.

THE GENERAL APPROACH

IN THE *ROYAL Diaries* case, Lord Phillips CJ said that the identification of a claimant's reasonable expectations involves a number of factors which form an 'interdependent amalgam of circumstances'.[1] No single factor is decisive. Thus, for example, even if there is a 'confidential relationship' of a classic kind between the claimant and the defendant, the question will still remain whether particular information is confidential—not every item of information communicated within such a relationship will be protected.[2] Each case must be decided 'on its own facts'.[3] In broad terms, however, the factors identified in the

[1] *HRH Prince of Wales v Associated Newspapers Ltd* [2006] EWCA Civ 1776, [2007] 3 WLR 222, [36].

[2] See, eg, *Lord Browne of Madingley v Associated Newspapers Ltd* [2007] EWCA Civ 295, [2007] 3 WLR 289, [29] and [32]; *Tillery Valley Foods v Channel Four Television* [2004] EWHC 1075 (Ch), *The Times*, 11 May 2004, [11] (Mann J) (not everything that happens in a workplace is confidential). In *Lord Browne's Case*, the CA gave the example of a husband telling his wife that Oxford or Cambridge won the boat race in a particular year as an instance of non-confidential information communicated within a confidential relationship.

[3] [2007] EWCA Civ 295, [2007] 3 WLR 289, [36].

cases fall into the four categories specified in § 2. The categories are not, of course, hermetically sealed from each other. Where the defendant is also a confidant, the categories often merge.

In deciding whether information is confidential to a claimant, courts consider the position from the perspective of the 'reasonable man',[4] the 'man of average intelligence and honesty',[5] the 'reasonable person of ordinary sensibilities',[6] or the 'sensibilities of a reasonable person placed in the situation of the subject of the disclosure'.[7] The approach, therefore, is ultimately objective. The aim is not so much to discover what the claimant in fact expected, as to fix, objectively, the limits of what she was entitled to expect.

RELATIONSHIPS

Although the existence of a confidential relationship between the claimant and a confidant (not necessarily the defendant, of course) is neither necessary nor in itself sufficient, it remains important. It will be easier to establish a reasonable expectation of confidentiality or privacy against the background of a 'confidential relationship' than between complete strangers. The cases establish a number of relationships which are regarded as confidential.

Many professional relationships[8] carry implied obligations of confidentiality as well-established incidents: doctors and patients,[9] bankers and their customers,[10] employees and their employers,[11] lawyers and their clients,[12] accountants and their clients,[13] estate agents and their clients,[14] clergy and members of their congregation.[15] Duties of confidentiality are also owed between parties to an arbitration[16] (and, presumably, by arbitrators), and in the context of a mediation.[17] In many cases, parties to commercial agreements will expressly include confidentiality provisions, and in others they will be implied.

The categories of confidential relationship, however, are not limited to relationships which involve (or are akin to) contract. The relationships between

[4] *Coco v A N Clark (Engineers) Ltd* [1969] RPC 41, 48 (Megarry J).

[5] *Printers & Finishers Ltd v Holloway* [1965] RPC 239, 257 (Cross J).

[6] *Australian Broadcasting Corp v Lenah Game Meats Pty Ltd* (2001) 208 CLR 199, [42] (Gleeson CJ), *Campbell v MGN Ltd* [2004] UKHL 22, [2004] 2 AC 457, [94] (Lord Hope).

[7] *Campbell v MGN Ltd* [2004] UKHL 22, [2004] 2 AC 457, at [136] (Baroness Hale).

[8] For further information see, generally, Toulson & Phipps, chs 11–16.

[9] *Hunter v Mann* [1974] QB 767, 772 (DC); *R v Mid Glamorgan Family Health Services, ex parte Martin* [1995] 1 WLR 110, 117 (Nourse LJ), 119 (Sir Roger Parker); *W v Egdell* [1990] Ch 359 (CA).

[10] *Tournier v National Provincial and Union Bank of England* [1924] 1 KB 461 (CA).

[11] See, eg, *Faccenda Chicken Ltd v Fowler* [1987] Ch 117 (CA).

[12] *Prince Jefri Bolkiah v KPMG* [1999] 2 AC 222 (HL), 235 (Lord Millett).

[13] *Ibid* (audit work), and generally (accountants acting as experts in litigation).

[14] *Kelly v Cooper* [1993] AC 205, 213 (PC).

[15] *Hunter v Mann* [1974] QB 767, 772 (DC).

[16] *Dolling Baker v Merrett* [1990] 1 WLR 1205 (CA).

[17] *Re D (Minors)* [1993] Fam 231 (CA), *Theodoropoulas v Theodoropoulas* [1964] P 311.

spouses,[18] lovers in a long-term relationship,[19] or close friends,[20] are all capable of being regarded as relevant to the existence and ambit of a duty of confidence.

INACCESSIBILITY

It is sometimes suggested that the means by which the defendant acquired the information is relevant to its confidentiality, so that if the defendant has resorted to reprehensible measures to obtain the information (deception, trespass, the use of surveillance equipment) it is more likely to be regarded as confidential.[21] This may well be true, in practical terms. But it is necessary to keep two questions distinct. On the one hand, there is the question whether the *claimant* had a reasonable expectation of privacy. On the other hand, there is the question whether the *defendant* had notice of that expectation. Where information has been acquired surreptitiously or clandestinely, that may help answer both questions—but for different reasons. The fact that such measures were taken may show that the information was kept in such a way as to limit its general availability.[22] That goes to the expectation of privacy. The fact that the defendant resorted to such measures may show that he understood that the information was expected to be inaccessible.[23] That goes to the question of notice. But the mere fact that the defendant happens to have made use of surreptitious or unlawful means to obtain the information does not make it confidential.[24] For instance, a person who sneaks into a football match without paying in order to watch the game obtains information surreptitiously, but the information does not thereby become confidential.

The key question, therefore, is whether information is private or confidential in the sense that (*a*) it is 'available to one person (or a group of persons) and not generally available to others' and (*b*) the person to whom it is available 'does not intend that it should become available to others'.[25] The 'form in which [the information] is kept'[26] may demonstrate that limitation on access and

[18] *Argyll v Argyll* [1967] Ch 302.

[19] *Lord Browne of Madingley v Associated Newspapers Ltd* [2007] EWCA Civ 295, [2007] 3 WLR 289; *Barrymore v News Group Newspapers Ltd* [1997] FSR 600, 603 (Jacob J). In *A v B plc* [2002] EWCA Civ 337, [2003] QB 195, the CA suggested that it was less likely that confidence would attach to a very short-term sexual relationship or isolated encounter. It seems correct to surmise that such matters are more likely to be protected because of the nature of the information (see n 38 below) than because of the relationship itself.

[20] *Stephens v Avery* [1988] Ch 449 (Browne-Wilkinson V-C); *McKennitt v Ash* [2006] EWCA Civ 1714, [2007] 3 WLR 194 (CA).

[21] See, *eg*, *Ashburton v Pape* [1913] 2 Ch 469 (CA), 475 (Swinfen Eady LJ).

[22] But that is not decisive. In *Mars UK Ltd v Teknowledge Ltd* [2000] FSR 138, information had been encrypted; but it was held not to be confidential. The decision seems questionable.

[23] See, *eg*, *Shelley Films Ltd v Rex Features Ltd* [1994] EMLR 134.

[24] In this respect at least—though not in its result—*Kaye v Robertson* [1991] FSR 62 (CA) remains correct: information *may* be obtained illegally or improperly, and yet not be subject to any duty of confidentiality.

[25] *Douglas v Hello! Ltd* (*No 3*) [2005] EWCA Civ 595, [2006] QB 125, [55].

[26] *Ibid*, [83].

the claimant's intentions and expectations in that respect. Thus the fact that the claimant has taken special steps to limit attendance at an event and to prevent those attending from taking photographs helps to demonstrate an intention that photographic information about the event should be confidential.[27]

Conversely, where the information in question is such as any member of the public might readily observe, or obtain by simple enquiry, it is less likely to be regarded as confidential. So, for example, where the claimant visited a brothel and might be observed entering it by any member of the public, that fact was not something in relation to which he had any reasonable expectation of privacy; but he would have had such an expectation in relation to the activities that took place in private there.[28] And if people choose to talk indiscreetly about their sexual affairs with strangers in a public bar, they are unlikely to be able to complain if their conversations are repeated.[29]

But one should not go too far by making secrecy-in-fact so important that it is the only factor. The mere fact that something is observable to the public does not make it 'fair game' to be widely published or repeated. Thus in *Peck v United Kingdom*[30] the European Court of Human Rights held that a person had an expectation of privacy which was violated when CCTV footage of him attempting suicide in public was broadcast. And in *von Hannover v Germany*[31] the European Court of Human Rights found a violation of Article 8 where photographs had been taken of the applicant and her family in the 'semi-public' environment of a restaurant. It is clear, then, that there may be an expectation of 'privacy' even in a 'public space',[32] particularly where what is in issue is not simply informative statements, but photographs or video recordings. English law now takes the same position. In *Campbell v MGN Ltd*,[33] the House of Lords held that photographs taken in a public street might be private.[34] Similarly, in *Jagger v Darling*[35] it was accepted that a person who had sex in a public place (a nightclub) was arguably owed a duty of confidence in relation to CCTV footage from the club. Since she had not realised that her conduct would be observed clearly or electronically recorded, she enjoyed a legitimate expectation of privacy.

By the same token, information may be distributed to a fairly wide group of people without losing its confidential character. In the *Royal Diaries* case, for

[27] *Douglas v Hello! Ltd (No 3)* [2007] UKHL 21, [2007] 2 WLR 920; *Shelley Films Ltd v Rex Features Ltd* [1994] EMLR 134; *Creation Records Ltd v News Group Newspapers Ltd* [1997] EMLR 444.

[28] *Theakston v Mirror Group Newspapers Ltd* [2002] EWHC 137, [2002] EMLR 22.

[29] *Shepherd v News Group Newspapers Ltd* (20 Mar 1998, Lindsay J), unreported but discussed in Tugendhat & Christie, 255.

[30] (2003) 36 EHRR 41.

[31] (2004) 40 EHRR 1.

[32] See generally, NA Moreham, 'Privacy in Public Places' [2006] *CLJ* 606.

[33] [2004] UKHL 22, [2004] 2 AC 457.

[34] See also *R v Broadcasting Standards Commission, ex parte British Broadcasting Corporation* [2001] QB 885 (CA).

[35] [2005] EWHC 683 (Ch).

instance, the Court of Appeal rejected the suggestion that by providing copies of private diaries to a number of people over the years, Prince Charles had demonstrated an intention that the contents should be publicly available.[36]

NATURE OF THE INFORMATION

Some sorts of subject-matter are inherently more likely to be regarded as private or confidential: most of us regard our sex lives and financial affairs as more sensitive than information about our taste in music—we are more circumspect in choosing confidants in relation to such matters, and expect a higher degree of discretion. It is also a reflection of the fact that such information is quite central to our sense of who we are, that sense of personal identity that it is the business of Article 8 of the Convention to protect.[37] The same is true of commercial or government information: some matters are inherently more likely to be regarded as secret than others.

Common sense is a useful guide here. Information about a person's sex life and close personal relationships is likely to be confidential.[38] So is information about a person's medical condition.[39] So is information about a person's personal financial circumstances.[40] Business information may be protected,[41] and of course very often is protected where the claimant is a business; that covers matters such as inventions, costs and prices if not generally known,[42] and the nature or appearance of future products. Where it is obvious that a document contains legal advice, it will be treated as confidential, and protected accordingly.[43] Information is more likely to be protected if it is specific and significant. Vague information, or information which contains nothing of novelty or commercial importance, is unlikely to be sensibly regarded as confidential, especially in a business context.[44]

[36] *HRH Prince of Wales v Associated Newspapers Ltd* [2006] EWCA Civ 1776, [2007] 3 WLR 222, [42]–[43].

[37] See, eg, *Niemietz v Germany* (1992) 16 EHRR 97, [29].

[38] *Dudgeon v United Kingdom* (1981) 4 EHRR 149; *Pierce v Governing Body of Mayfields School* [2001] IRLR 669, [15] (Hale LJ: 'sexual behaviour is . . . a most intimate and important part of private life'); *A v B plc* [2002] EWCA Civ 337, [2003] QB 195; *X & Y v Persons Unknown* [2006] EWHC 2783 (QB), [2007] HRLR 4 (state of claimants' marriage); *CC v AB* [2006] EWHC 3083 (QB), [2007] EMLR 312, [8]; *Lord Browne of Madingley v Associated Newspapers Ltd* [2007] EWHC 202 (QB).

[39] *Campbell v MGN Ltd* [2004] UKHL 22, [2004] 2 AC 457; *Venables v News Group Newspapers Ltd* [2001] Fam 430, [81]; *R v Department of Health, ex parte Source Informatics Ltd* [2001] QB 424 (CA).

[40] *Australian Broadcasting Corp v Lenah Game Meats Pty Ltd* (2001) 208 CLR 199, [42] (Gleeson CJ).

[41] *Lord Browne of Madingley v Associated Newspapers Ltd* [2007] EWCA Civ 295, [2007] 3 WLR 289, [34].

[42] *Herbert Morris Ltd v Saxelby* [1916] 1 AC 688 (HL), 705 (Lord Atkinson).

[43] *English & American Insurance Co v Herbert Smith* [1988] FSR 232 (Browne-Wilkinson J).

[44] *De Maudsley v Palumbo* [1996] FSR 447, 456 (Knox J). It has often been pointed out, however, that the combination of known ideas may be a valuable novelty: *Coco v A N Clark (Engineers) Ltd* [1969] RPC 41, 47 (Megarry J) is the classic statement: 'Novelty depends on the thing itself, not upon

Apart from subject-matter, a second question concerns the form of the information. Form matters, and 'information' (broadly described) which may not be confidential in one form may be confidential in another. For instance, if information is compiled into easily usable form, the compilation may be confidential although the underlying information is not. Thus, although the identity of a firm's customers is not itself confidential,[45] a customer list in which that information is set out may be.[46] Similarly, information conveyed in words may be treated differently from information conveyed in photographs or film.[47] Information that is so successfully anonymized that the person concerned cannot be identified may not be subject to any duty of confidence at all.[48] The precise form and details of the information therefore matter.

Thirdly, attention will be paid to the consequences for the individual concerned if the information is disclosed, and the vulnerability of the individual. Information whose disclosure may have serious consequences for the individual concerned—for instance by exposing her to physical or psychological harm—is more likely to be regarded as private (because it must be kept private to protect rights under Article 8 of the Convention).[49] And where a person is vulnerable—for instance because of a mental illness—it is more likely that conduct will be regarded as private, even though it takes place in a place to which the public have access.[50]

PROVISION OF INFORMATION FOR LIMITED PURPOSES

Where information is provided for limited purposes—for example to the police for the purposes of detecting crime[51]—there is often an expectation that it will be used for the proper purposes only. That is especially true where the informa-

the quality of its constituent parts.' Novelty, moreover, is not essential; although it may be a factor in 'trade secret' cases, information may be confidential without being novel. See, eg, *Cadbury Schweppes Inc v FBI Foods Ltd* [2000] FSR 491, [65] (Binnie J) (assessment of damages for the use of information that is 'nothing special').

[45] *Suhner & Co AG v Transradio Ltd* [1967] RPC 329, 333 (Plowman J).

[46] *Robb v Green* [1895] 2 QB 315 (CA).

[47] *Campbell v MGN Ltd* [2004] UKHL 22, [2004] 2 AC 457, [123] (Lord Hope) and [155] (Baroness Hale); *Douglas v Hello! Ltd (No 3)* [2005] EWCA Civ 595, [2006] QB 125, [84]–[90].

[48] *R v Department of Health, ex parte Source Informatics Ltd* [2001] QB 424 (CA) (anonymised patient information). Contrast *X v Y* [1988] 2 All ER 648 where, although the information was anonymous, it was likely that from other information the individuals concerned would be capable of being identified.

[49] *Venables v News Group Newspapers Ltd* [2001] Fam 430. Contrast *Mahmood v Galloway* [2006] EWHC 1286 (QB), [22] (no risk of serious harm established). In *Nicholls v British Broadcasting Corp* [1999] EMLR 791 (CA) the existence of an arguable duty of confidence was conceded in relation to a police informer whose life was said to be at risk from identification.

[50] See *Peck v United Kingdom* (2003) 36 EHRR 41.

[51] See, eg, *Marcel v Commissioner of Police of the Metropolis* [1992] Ch 225 (CA); *Woolgar v Chief Constable of Sussex Police* [2000] 1 WLR 26 (CA), 29 (Kennedy LJ); *Hellewell v Chief Constable of Derbyshire* [1995] 1 WLR 804.

tion is provided under compulsion—for instance pursuant to a court order[52]—or under the threat of compulsion.[53] The same applies, in principle, to information provided voluntarily to a public authority, or to information provided privately by one individual to another for a specific purpose.[54]

The difficulty, particularly in cases involving the exercise of statutory powers, is to give a proper definition of the purpose. The danger is normally in assuming too narrow a range of purposes. Thus, for instance, in *R v Licensing Authority Established Under Medicines Act 1968, ex parte Smith Kline & French Laboratories Ltd*[55] the purpose for which the applicant for a licence provided information was to enable the authority to decide whether or not to license a product. But the statutory scheme made it legitimate for the authority to use the information not only for that purpose but also in discharging other statutory functions. The test, in other words, is not simply the purpose or objective that the person providing the information may have had, but the purposes which that person ought objectively to have contemplated, having regard to the relevant statutory scheme. In purely private cases, where the purpose for which information is provided is not determined by any statutory rules, the question must be answered in all the circumstances of the case.

[52] See, eg, CPR 31.22, which restricts the use of documents disclosed in litigation.

[53] *Re Barlow Clowes Gilt Managers Ltd* [1992] Ch 208, 217 (Millett J).

[54] See, eg, *Saltman Engineering Co Ltd v Campbell Engineering Co Ltd* (1948) 65 RPC 203 (CA), 213 (Lord Greene MR); *Barrymore v News Group Newspapers Ltd* [1997] FSR 600, 602 (Jacob J). See also Gurry, 113, where it is described as 'the general test', and many other authorities are collected. In view of the developments in the law since 1984, Gurry's emphasis on this factor above all others is probably too great, but it undoubtedly remains important.

[55] [1990] 1 AC 64 (HL).

§ 3

False Information

Information may be protected even if it is false.

IT MIGHT AT first sight seem that there is a clear dividing line between wrongs whose essential characteristic is that the defendant has said or written something false (defamation and malicious falsehood), and breach of confidence. In the normal case, the information the claimant wishes to protect by an action for breach of confidence is true—that is the very nub of the claimant's concern. The claimant wants to keep a secret, even a disreputable or embarrassing secret.

It is of course correct that truth is no defence to an action for breach of confidence: a claimant may fail to establish defamation (because the defendant proves a defence of justification) and yet still succeed if the information was disclosed in breach of confidence.[1] But does it follow that 'information' cannot be confidential if it is untrue?

In principle the answer is, No. Suppose, for instance, that in the course of treatment a patient is tested for HIV, and the test is positive. The doctor discloses what she believes to be the patient's HIV status to the press. Clearly, an action for breach of confidence lies. It can make no difference that the test has yielded a *false* positive result. Or suppose the press obtain intelligence that a celebrity has been seen having sex in a hotel with a mistress, and publish a story about it. Can it make any difference that the celebrity in question was actually having sex with his wife? The examples can be multiplied—for instance if publication were of details of one disease whereas in fact the claimant suffers from another, and so forth. Intuitively, in none of these cases ought it to make any difference that the information is not accurate.[2]

The case law now confirms (after initial hesitation[3]) that information may be protected even though it is false. Thus the claimant will not be required to pick

[1] See, eg, *Cornelius v de Taranto* [2001] EWCA Civ 1511, [2002] EMLR 6, in which the claimant recovered damages for the communication, in breach of confidence, of a defamatory (but justified) report.

[2] The intuition is shared by Toulson & Phipps, para 3–094.

[3] *Khashoggi v Smith* (1980) 124 SJ 149 (CA); *Interbrew SA v Financial Times Ltd* [2002] EWCA Civ 274, [2002] 2 Lloyd's Rep 229, [38]–[39], where (however) the proposition that there could be no confidence in false information seems to have been conceded.

through a long account, partly true and partly false, to separate the true from the false.[4] In *McKennitt v Ash*, the Court of Appeal went further, holding that:

> provided the matter complained of is by its nature such as to attract the law of breach of confidence, then the defendant cannot deprive the claimant of his article 8 protection simply by demonstrating that the matter is untrue.[5]

This is all very well in theory. But in practice there can be an air of unreality about asking whether the claimant had any 'expectation of confidentiality' with respect to false information. Does a straight footballer, for example, reasonably expect his homosexuality to be kept confidential?[6] This might be thought almost a meaningless question. Such a person probably has no expectation that his *sexuality* is confidential (he may be married, or have well-publicised girlfriends: he is happy for the world to know that he is straight). He has no expectation with regard to his *homo*sexuality, since he is not gay. And the question 'What *would* his expectation be if he were gay?' is close to unanswerable: some public figures are happy for the world to know that they are gay; others are not.

It may matter. For by putting a case as one of breach of confidence rather than defamation or malicious falsehood, a claimant might seek to avoid various substantive and procedural rules which tend to protect defendants in the traditional torts protecting reputation—such as proof of malice, or of damage to reputation, or the one-year limitation period applicable to defamation and malicious falsehood,[7] or the residual right to trial by jury.[8] The risk that claimants might circumvent the protections built into these specialised areas of law militates against too readily extending the law of confidentiality to protect dissemination of false information.

Without further case law, it is impossible to be sure how these conundrums will be solved. For present purposes it is suggested that there are at least two (overlapping) categories of information that will clearly be protected, but that it is questionable how far protection will extend outside these two categories.

First, false information is protected when it has in fact been learned by the defendant (as true) in the course of a confidential relationship. Thus if the claimant tells the defendant something confidentially, there is a duty of confidence even if the information is false.[9] But the principle extends beyond what is said, to all information learned (as true) by the defendant in a confidential relationship, and to the opinions or conclusions drawn by the defendant as inferences from that information. Thus diagnoses made by a doctor on the basis

[4] *McKennitt v Ash* [2005] EWHC 3003 (QB), [2006] EMLR 10, [78].

[5] *McKennitt v Ash* [2006] EWCA Civ 1714, [2007] 3 WLR 194, [80] (Buxton LJ). See also *W v Westminster City Council* [2005] EWHC 102 (QB), noted but not on this point [2005] 4 All ER 96.

[6] Taking the facts of a case that occurred in 2006, when *The Sun* apologised to a premiership footballer, Ashley Cole, in relation to such conduct.

[7] Limitation Act 1980, s 4A. For discussion of ways in which this problem might be resolved, see § 26 below.

[8] Supreme Court Act 1981, s 69 (1) (b).

[9] For instance, if a client were to 'confess' to his lawyer that he was guilty of a crime that he had not in fact committed. The confession is still confidential.

of tests and observations are confidential, whether or not they are correct. So are opinions formed by a banker about the customer's activities and lifestyle, based on activity on the account.

Secondly, false information is protected if its inherent nature is such that one can clearly say that, if it were true, there would be an expectation of confidentiality in the absence of express consent to publish or use it. That would cover, for instance, intimate details about a person's private life or close relationships. It appears to be what Buxton LJ had in mind when he spoke of information that is 'by its nature' confidential. It is information that one is entitled to assume would have been subject to a duty of confidence if it had been true.

Accepting that false information may be protected where those principles apply leaves more difficult cases for resolution as they occur. In particular, it does not dictate what should happen (*a*) if one person in a confidential relationship simply invents a falsehood about the other person (ie, if the information does not in fact originate in anything communicated within the relationship)[10] or (*b*) if somebody communicates false information which is in a 'grey area' where its confidentiality is heavily dependent upon the attitude taken by the person to whom it relates. In either case, some remedy may well lie—but it seems open to argument that the proper remedy should be for defamation or malicious falsehood, and not for breach of confidence.

[10] This, or something like it, seems to have been the position in *Interbrew SA v Financial Times Ltd* [2002] EWCA Civ 274, [2002] 2 Lloyd's Rep 279, where a confidential document had been deliberately altered to contain a '"lethal cocktail" of fact and falsehood'.

§ 4

Agreement

A defendant will be held to have agreed to keep information confidential where, on an objective view of the communications and conduct of the parties, he has done so, regardless of his subjective intentions.

IN *SPYCATCHER*[1] LORD Goff made it clear that there are two alternative ways in which a defendant is held bound by an obligation of confidence: (*a*) where he has agreed, or is held to have agreed, to be so bound and (*b*) where he has sufficient notice that the information in question is confidential, regardless of agreement. This section is concerned only with the first of those possibilities. The second is addressed in § 5.

An 'agreement' in this context need not be a contractual agreement. Often there will be a contract (for instance, between employer and employee). But sometimes there may be a sufficiently consensual relationship to warrant treating confidentiality as based on agreement even though there is no contract as such (for instance, between barristers and their lay clients). It may be a matter of chance whether a particular relationship is contractual in the strict sense. For example, whereas the relationship between a private doctor and his patient is contractual, the relationship between an NHS doctor and his patient is not. Nevertheless, in both cases, the duty of confidence would be regarded as arising consensually, based on agreement, and the principles in this section would be applied. So too, probably, in cases where the relationship is non-economic and clearly incapable of being contractual—for instance between clergy and their congregation or between spouses or friends.

It is a general principle of English contract law that questions of agreement—whether there is an agreement and what its terms are—are decided objectively. They depend on the external manifestations of consensus, objectively interpreted, and not on the parties' private thoughts.[2] The same principle is applied

[1] *Attorney-General v Guardian Newspapers (No 2)* [1990] 1 AC 109 (HL), 281.

[2] See generally Beale (ed), *Chitty on Contracts*, 29th edn (London, 2004), Vol. 1, paras 2–001 and 5–056; M Furmston (ed), *The Law of Contract,* 3rd edn (London, 2007), paras 2.145–2.154. Leading cases include *Smith v Hughes* (1871) LR 6 QB 597 (CA) and *Paal Wilson & Co A/S v Partenreederei Hannah Blumenthal* (*The Hannah Blumenthal*) [1983] 1 AC 854 (HL).

by equity.[3] There is no reason why any different approach should be taken to the question whether a defendant has agreed to keep particular information confidential. As Bingham LJ expressed it:

> Where the relationship . . . is contractual, the question is whether the [confidant's] disclosure is a or is not a breach of contract. The answer to that question must turn not on what the [confidant] thinks, but on what the court rules.[4]

The confidant's professional judgment may be relevant in assisting the court to reach its conclusion, but it is not decisive. Interpretation is objective. It is:

> the ascertainment of the meaning which the document would convey to a reasonable person having all the background knowledge which would reasonably have been available to the parties in the situation in which they were at the time of the contract.[5]

In some cases that will involve interpretation of an express confidentiality agreement. In others it will involve the implication of terms based on what are understood to have been the common expectations of the parties to a particular relationship, or the established legal incidents of a particular relationship, or the terms that are necessary in order to give business efficacy to that relationship. It is in precisely this way that the obligations of confidentiality that are understood to be implicit in many types of commercial and professional relationship have been developed and established.[6] The whole matter is thoroughly objective.

Once it is held that a person agreed to keep information confidential as a matter of construction (or implication), that obligation will generally be enforced regardless of the subjective state of mind of the defendant. In other words, a defendant who is held to have agreed to keep information confidential will generally be kept to that agreement, and may be held in breach of it even if he believed that he was doing nothing wrong. The obligations are, in that sense, likely to be 'strict'—they are not dependent on any element of subjective bad faith on the part of the defendant. The fact that the defendant has honestly attempted to comply with what he perceives are his obligations is irrelevant.[7]

THE SIGNIFICANCE OF CONTRACT

As set out above, in general it seems to make no difference whether consensual obligations of confidentiality are derived from the terms of a contract as such or not. In most cases, the terms implied in a contract and the terms that would be

[3] *Bank of Credit and Commerce International SA v Ali* [2001] UKHL 8, [2002] 1 AC 251, [25] (Lord Nicholls).

[4] *W v Egdell* [1990] 1 Ch 359 (CA), 422.

[5] *Investors Compensation Scheme Ltd v West Bromwich Building Society* [1998] 1 WLR 896 (HL), 912 (Lord Hoffman).

[6] See above, pp 8 to 9.

[7] See, eg, *Prince Jefri Bolkiah v KPMG* [1999] 2 AC 222 (HL), where the defendant believed that it had put in place sufficient 'chinese walls' to prevent breach of the duty of confidence, but the court disagreed.

treated as applying as incidents of a non-contractual relationship are essentially the same. Whether the case is put 'in contract' or 'in confidence' makes no practical difference.

The existence of a contract, however, is not always irrelevant. Where there is an actual contract, the courts' usual preference seems to be to treat the obligations under the contract as determinative. It is not thought necessary or desirable to rely on some equitable supplement to the contract, but rather the obligations of confidentiality are treated as (and by reference to) the express or implied terms of the contract. The contract governs, and contractual analysis dominates.[8]

The contract and its terms may expand or restrict the ambit of the ordinary duties of confidence that equity would regard as applicable to a particular situation. Thus the parties may expressly agree to keep confidential information which equity would not normally regard as confidential,[9] thereby expanding the scope of the duty. Such expansions are not always unproblematic: they may give rise to questions of public policy.[10] For instance, an express agreement to keep information about intended criminal conduct secret would violate the public policy that information may be disclosed to prevent crime.[11] And an employee's agreement never to use some types of confidential information might violate the common law policy against restraint of trade.[12] There may also be questions about the extent to which relief ought to be given where the information in question would not normally be regarded as confidential. But, subject to such wrinkles, there seems to be no principled reason why persons should not enter into contractually enforceable agreements to keep *anything* confidential, however silly they may seem. And express contractual duties *may* carry more weight than implied duties or common law duties when balancing interests in confidentiality against other interests (for instance in freedom of expression).[13]

Just as a contract may expressly expand protection to information which would not be protected if the parties had been silent about it, so it may remove protection which would otherwise have been available. It is always possible for a potential claimant to agree (contractually or otherwise) to permit disclosure or use of information which would normally be regarded as confidential. Little difficulty arises where the agreement is express. But it may also be implied. As with fiduciary duties,[14] it should not be assumed that equitable duties of confidence arising from agreement are always the same. They must be responsive to their contractual context, which may show that the parties have impliedly

[8] See, in particular *Faccenda Chicken Ltd v Fowler* [1987] Ch 117, 135 (CA); *Vokes Ltd v Heather* (1945) 62 RPC 135 (CA), 136, 141 (Lord Greene MR).

[9] See, eg, *Attorney-General v Barker* [1990] 3 All ER 256 (CA).

[10] Though the suggestion of Lord Denning MR in *Dunford & Elliott Ltd v Johnson and Firth Brown Ltd* [1978] FSR 143 (CA), 148, that the courts should decline to enforce unreasonable stipulations of confidentiality seems to go too far.

[11] See § 12.

[12] See § 16.

[13] *Campbell v Frisbee* [2002] EWCA Civ 1375, [2003] ICR 141, [25]. See further below, p 56.

[14] *Henderson v Merrett Syndicates Ltd* [1995] 2 AC 145 (HL), 206 (Lord Browne-Wilkinson).

agreed to permit a confidant to use information in a way that might normally be impermissible.[15] And, although broadly similar, the duties are not identical in all cases: what is expected of a lawyer, for instance, is not exactly what is expected of a doctor.

THE EFFECT OF REPUDIATORY BREACH

Where confidentiality rests on a contractual agreement, what happens if the contract is brought to an end because one party repudiates it? The point arises most often in employment cases, where confidentiality obligations are regarded as primarily contractual, and where repudiatory breach by the employer (in the form of wrongful dismissal) is not uncommon.

One possibility is that a repudiatory breach (once it is accepted) brings to an end *all* unexecuted obligations. This was the view of the House of Lords in *General Billposting Co Ltd v Atkinson*,[16] which concerned the enforcement of a restrictive covenant after dismissal. But, however convincing that view may have appeared in 1909, by the 1990s its correctness seemed open to question. As Phillips LJ pointed out in *Rock Refrigeration Ltd v Jones*,[17] the law of contract has moved on in various ways since 1909. In particular, it has been recognised that there can be contractual terms (for example, arbitration agreements,[18] jurisdiction clauses,[19] and provisions limiting the damages recoverable for breach of contract[20]) which will survive the termination of the substantive or primary obligations of the contract. The underlying premise of *General Billposting*, namely that repudiation justifies the wronged party in 'rescinding the contract and treating himself as absolved from the further performance of it on his part',[21] now seems too simple—for it is now understood that termination for breach is not the same thing as rescission *ab initio*,[22] and that it does not even necessarily entail the discharge of all contractual obligations.

The rule in *General Billposting* probably still applies to restrictive covenants, properly so called; it was so applied by the Court of Appeal in *Rock Refrigeration*, and it seems likely that (short of the House of Lords) it remains applicable in that specific context. It is, however, likely—though not certain[23]—

15 *Kelly v Cooper* [1993] AC 205 (PC).
16 [1909] AC 118.
17 [1998] ICR 938 (CA), 958–60.
18 *Heyman v Darwins Ltd* [1942] AC 356 (HL); *Bremer Vulkan Schiffbau und Maschinenfabrik v South India Shipping Corp* [1981] AC 909 (HL); *Harbour Assurance Co (UK) Ltd v Kansa General International Insurance Co Ltd* [1993] 1 Lloyd's Rep 455 (CA). See now Arbitration Act 1996, s 7.
19 *Mackender v Feldia AG* [1967] 2 QB 590 (CA).
20 *Photo Productions Ltd v Securicor Transport Ltd* [1980] AC 827 (HL).
21 [1909] AC 118, 122 (Lord Collins).
22 *Johnson v Agnew* [1980] AC 367 (HL), 393 (Lord Wilberforce).
23 See *Campbell v Frisbee* [2002] EWCA Civ 1375, [2003] ICR 141, [22]. In *Hyde Park Residence Ltd v Yelland* [2001] Ch 143 (CA), [74], Mance LJ seems to have assumed that repudiation *does* discharge obligations of confidence; but the observations are *obiter* and the point does not appear to have been argued fully.

that duties to respect confidential information may survive termination,[24] even termination as a result of breach by the confidant. This was the conclusion expressed (albeit *obiter*) by Morritt LJ in *Rock Refrigeration*,[25] and by Lightman J at first instance in *Campbell v Frisbee*.[26]

[24] Post-termination duties may be narrower than pre-termination ones, however, particularly in employment contracts: see § 16.

[25] [1998] ICR 938, 953.

[26] [2002] EWHC 328 (Ch); [2002] EMLR 656. The Court of Appeal [2002] EWCA Civ 1375, [2003] ICR 141, thought that Lightman J's conclusion had been too confident for the purposes of granting summary judgment, but did not express a positive view to the contrary.

§ 5

Notice

A defendant who has not agreed to keep information confidential will have notice of its confidentiality sufficient to impose an obligation of confidence if, at the time of publication or use,—

(a) the defendant actually knows that the information is confidential,
(b) it is obvious that the information is confidential, but the defendant wilfully shuts his eyes to that fact, or
(c) on the facts as they are known to the defendant, a reasonable person would know that the information is confidential.

A CONTROVERSIAL ISSUE

IN *SPYCATCHER*[1] LORD Goff referred to the defendant who had 'notice . . . that the information is confidential'. But he did not explain what he meant, in this context, by 'notice'. Indeed, he pointed out that he had 'used the word "notice" advisedly, in order to avoid the . . . question of the extent to which actual knowledge is necessary.'[2] That question, however, must be grappled with. Unfortunately the answers given in the cases are not consistent or clear.

There is no doubt about § 5 (*a*) or (*b*). A defendant who actually knows that information is confidential will be bound to respect that confidentiality. And (as generally with questions of knowledge) a defendant who wilfully shuts his eyes to what is obvious is in no better position than someone with actual knowledge.[3] It is important, however, to understand that obviousness *alone* is not enough to meet the standard for 'blind eye' knowledge set out in § 5 (*b*): it must be accompanied by a state of wilful indifference on the part of the defendant, so

[1] *Attorney-General v Guardian Newspapers* (*No 2*) [1990] 1 AC 109, 281.
[2] *Ibid.*
[3] *Ibid.* For the general position see, eg, *Emerald Construction Co Ltd v Lowthian* [1966] 1 WLR 691 (CA).

that an honest but extremely careless misunderstanding of the position does not suffice.[4] If careless misunderstanding is to count, it must be under § 5 (*c*).

The controversial question concerns § 5 (*c*), and the extent to which there is any truly objective element to the doctrine of notice in this context, or any element of 'constructive notice'. Here three lines of authority diverge.

The first line of authority insists on a high subjective standard of knowledge—indeed, requires the defendant to have a state of mind that may be characterised as 'dishonest'. A second line of authority applies what seems to be a purely objective standard, treating the defendant as having notice where the reasonable person in the defendant's position would have understood the information to be confidential. A third line of authority takes an intermediate position, including an objective element, but requiring that the position should be (objectively) obvious.

THE VARIOUS SITUATIONS

To make sense of the difficulties, it is helpful to consider a variety of different situations in which the defendant's obligation depends on notice. (*a*) *D* acquires the information about *C* without any communication as such—for instance by direct observation. (*b*) *C* communicates confidential information to *D*, but in circumstances where it is not possible to say that *D* has agreed to keep the information confidential. For instance, *C* communicates the information to *D* accidentally or by mistake. The inadvertent disclosure of a privileged document provides a classic example. (*c*) *C* confides information to *X* in circumstances where *X* owes *C* a duty of confidence (for instance, by agreement). In breach of that duty *X* imparts the information to *D*.

Information obtained directly. Where the defendant obtains information directly—for example by taking a photograph of the claimant, or by some device such as eavesdropping—it seems to be clearly established that the relevant test is essentially objective. The argument for such a standard was first made by Gurry,[5] and now[6] rests on the decision of the Court of Appeal and the House of Lords in *Campbell v MGN Ltd*.[7] There the Court of Appeal expressly rejected the application of an 'honesty' test in the context of a direct claim for invasion of privacy, and applied an objective test. It was held that the press

[4] *OBG Ltd v Allan* [2007] UKHL 21, [2007] 2 WLR 920, [69].

[5] Gurry, 115–20, 261–5, 273.

[6] For some, albeit equivocal, earlier support see *London & Provincial Sporting News Agency v Levy* (1928) [1923–28] *MacGillivray's Copyright Cases* 340, 341 (which might, however, be taken as a case of 'blind eye' knowledge). In *Union Carbide Corp v Naturin Ltd* [1987] FSR 538 (CA), 549, Slade LJ left the question undecided, but doubted whether a purely subjective test was correct. An objective test was also preferred in *De Maudsley v Palumbo* [1996] FSR 447 (Knox J) and *Valeo Vision SA v Flexible Lamps Ltd* [1995] RPC 205, 228 (Aldous J).

[7] [2002] EWCA Civ 1373, [2003] QB 663; reversed, but not on this point, [2004] UKHL 22, [2004] 2 AC 457.

could 'fairly be expected to identify confidential information about an individual's life which, absent good reason, it will be offensive to publish.'[8] Those members of the House of Lords who expressed a view seem also to have adopted an objective standard. Lord Nicholls said that the duty of confidence was imposed wherever a person came into possession of information which he 'knows *or ought to know*' is fairly and reasonably to be regarded as confidential (emphasis added).[9] Lord Hoffman said that equity imposes a duty of confidence on anyone who receives confidential information with 'actual *or constructive*' knowledge of its confidentiality (emphasis added).[10] There was no challenge to the Court of Appeal's basic approach to the issue.

Information communicated by the claimant. There is a clutch of cases that concern the inadvertent or mistaken disclosure of privileged information by one party to another in the context of litigation—starting (in modern times) with the decision in *English & American Insurance Co v Herbert Smith.*[11] The court asks whether a reasonable solicitor would have appreciated that the information had been disclosed inadvertently (and therefore without the intention of removing its confidential character).[12] That is an objective test.[13] It is, in a sense, a relaxed objective test because the court only intervenes where the disclosure is an 'obvious' error, and does not require the recipient to make inquiries to remove possible doubts.[14] But the fact that the defendant is entitled to take the benefit of doubts is not surprising, given the caution traditionally recognised about imposing over-rigorous standards in commercial contexts where quick and decisions are necessary. The test certainly remains objective, and there is no need to show that the recipient has acted in any way dishonestly.[15]

Receipt of information from third party communicating it in breach of confidence. It is in the cases where *X* communicates *C*'s confidential information to *D* wrongfully that the trouble has occurred. Toulson and Phipps[16] have suggested that such cases involve a form of 'accessory liability' by *D* for *X*'s breach of confidence. Starting from that observation, they have suggested that the correct analogy is to accessory liability for dishonest assistance in the misappropriation of trust property—where the relevant standard is one of subjective 'dishonesty'.[17]

8 [2002] EWCA Civ 1373, [2003] QB 663, [68].

9 [2004] UKHL 22, [2004] 2 AC 457, [14.

10 *Ibid,* [44]–[45].

11 [1988] FSR 232.

12 *Al Fayed v Commissioner of Police for the Metropolis* [2002] EWCA Civ 780; *Breeze v John Stacy* [2000] CP Rep 77 (CA); *International Business Machines Corp v Phoenix International (Computers) Ltd* [1995] 1 All ER 413.

13 *Al Fayed v Commissioner of Police for the Metropolis* [2002] EWCA Civ 780, [21].

14 *Breeze v John Stacy* [2000] CP Rep 77 (CA).

15 See also *Smith Kline & French Laboratories (Australia) Ltd v Department of Community Services* [1990] FSR 617, 647, where Gummow J adopted an objective test.

16 Toulson & Phipps, paras 3–067 to 3–068.

17 *Barlow Clowes International Ltd v Eurotrust International Ltd* [2005] UKPC 37, [2006] 1 WLR 1476; *Twinsectra Ltd v Yardley* [2002] UKHL 12, [2002] 2 AC 164; *Royal Brunei Airlines Sdn. Bhd. v Tan* [1995] 2 AC 378 (PC).

A subjective test found some first instance support,[18] and was adopted by a two-judge Court of Appeal in *Thomas v Pearce*.[19] In that case the defendant had been given customer information by a new employee brought from a former employer. She had made use of customer information, but (as the trial judge found) without giving any thought to the question whether it was proper to do so. It was held that she was not liable.

It is suggested that the 'dishonesty' test is wrong, and its adoption in *Thomas v Pearce* (without comprehensive citation or discussion of authority) was an unfortunate mistake.

Toulson and Phipps take as their starting point the proposition that in a 'three party' situation the defendant is held liable as an 'accessory' to the third party's breach. In most cases, however, that is not a correct analysis. The question is not whether *D* should be liable for *X*'s wrong, but whether *D* ever fell under a duty *of his own*. It is not an essential part of the cause of action to show that *D* assisted, or procured, or induced *X* to breach a duty of confidence—or even to show that X acted in breach of duty at all.[20] The *duty* owed by a person who acquires information from a wrongdoer is no more accessory than the duty of a person who acquires the information directly, or from the confidant herself.

It would be bizarre indeed if the person who acquired information from a third party who was acting in breach of confidence was in a better position than someone who acquired information directly or without any breach by a third party. If a duty is imposed on a direct acquirer based on (objective) notice—as it clearly is—there is no reason why the 'dishonesty' standard should apply to the person who acquires the information from a third party who happens to be acting wrongfully in communicating it.[21]

Indeed, if an analogy were needed, it ought not to be to the standard by which equity holds a person liable as an accessory for assisting in a breach of trust, or even to the arguably different standard that applies to hold a person who 'receives' trust property liable for the full value received,[22] but rather to the approach equity takes to the duties owed by a person with respect to trust

[18] *Carflow Products (UK) Ltd v Linwood Securities (Birmingham) Ltd* [1996] FSR 424, 428, where Jacobs J preferred a subjective view because 'equity looks to the conscience of the individual'. He noted, however, that it made no difference on the facts of *Carflow*.

[19] [2000] FSR 718 (CA).

[20] Of course, if the claimant chose to complain not of *D*'s use of the information, but that *D* had induced *X* to communicate the information, then the case *would* be one of accessory liability. Were it so it would be necessary to show that *D*'s inducement to X was carried out with the knowledge that *X*'s act would be a breach of duty. Such was the case alleged, and such the result, in *British Industrial Plastics Ltd v Ferguson* [1940] 1 All ER 479 (HL). It does not follow that most 'three-party' cases are to be so regarded.

[21] See, to similar effect, the views of Richard Arnold, 'Circumstances Importing an Obligation of Confidence' (2003) 119 *LQR* 193.

[22] *Bank of Credit and Commerce International (Overseas) Ltd v Akindele* [2001] Ch 437 (CA) (knowledge not dishonesty relevant to claim against recipient of trust property) (disapproved, but not on this point, in *Criterion Properties plc v Stratford UK Properties LLC* [2004] UKHL 28, [2004] 1 WLR 1846).

property that he receives and holds. In *Goddard v Nationwide Building Society*[23] and in the course of the *Spycatcher* litigation[24] Nourse LJ suggested that a person who acquires confidential information, like a person who acquires trust property, takes it subject to the equities unless she is a bona fide purchaser without notice, including constructive notice. That probably goes too far, since information is not property, and the acquirer who obtains information without any notice of confidentiality is free to use it as she wishes whether or not she has *purchased* it. But as an analogy it comes closer to the heart of the matter than the false analogy to accessory liability. The question in both cases is not whether *D* should be liable for a wrong done by a third party to the claimant (as it is in the accessory cases), but whether *D* should now be free to deal with property or information that *D* has acquired, without regard to C's rights and interests. In answering that question, equity does *not* apply a standard merely of honesty, but a more objective standard which includes constructive notice.

That should also lay to rest the proposition that because equity acts 'on the conscience' it must require subjective dishonesty.[25] As a general proposition, it does not withstand scrutiny. In many fields, equity is willing to intervene to protect a claimant even where the defendant has acted in perfect (subjective) good faith, so that constructive notice suffices to justify intervention. Given that this is clearly the position where confidential information is acquired directly or without any breach of duty by a third party, there is no cogent reason why it should not be the case where there does happen to be such a breach. The true position is that stated by Gummow J in *Smith Kline & French*:

> [E]quity may impose an obligation of confidence upon a defendant having regard not only to what the defendant knew, but to what he ought to have known in all the relevant circumstances.[26]

A number of other points could be advanced against the 'dishonesty' standard. 'Dishonest' is not a word most people would readily apply to dealing with information. The meaning of the standard (and in particular whether the defendant must subjectively appreciate that his conduct is dishonest) is contested even in the field within which the test was developed.[27] Dishonesty therefore hardly offers a clear or workable test. But these points are really subsidiary. The stronger and better point is that given the very clear statements of high

[23] [1987] QB 670 (CA), 685.

[24] *Attorney-General v Observer Ltd*, unreported, 25 Jul 1986, quoted by Lord Donaldson MR in *Attorney-General v Guardian Newspapers Ltd (No 2)* [1990] 1 AC 109, 177.

[25] The point that Jacobs J found attractive in *Carflow Products (UK) Ltd v Linwood Securities (Birmingham) Ltd* [1996] FSR 424, 428.

[26] *Smith Kline & French Laboratories (Australia) Ltd v Department of Community Services* [1990] FSR 617, 649.

[27] It is unclear whether a person is to be treated as 'dishonest' in equity where he believes he is acting properly but, on the facts as he knows them, a reasonable person would think his conduct dishonest: compare *Barlow Clowes International Ltd v Eurotrust International Ltd* [2005] UKPC 37, [2006] 1 WLR 476 with *Twinsectra Ltd* v *Yardley* [2002] UKHL 12, [2002] 2 AC 164; and see *Abou-Rahmah v Abacha* [2006] EWCA Civ 1492, [2007] 1 Lloyd's Rep 115.

authority to the effect that whether a person has notice that information is confidential is, in other areas, an objective question there is no reason to apply a different standard in three-party situations where the source of the information happens to be acting in breach of confidence.

In fairness to the Court of Appeal which decided *Thomas v Pearce*,[28] it was not perhaps so clear, before *Campbell*, that in general the test ought to be objective.[29] Now that it is clear, however, *Thomas v Pearce* ought to be regarded as wrongly decided, and the beguiling but incorrect categorisation of three-party cases as involving some form of 'accessory' liability ought to be abandoned. Notice must be understood to include constructive notice.

It does not, however, follow that the doctrine of constructive notice ought to be too rigorously applied in this field. It appears to be sufficient if the defendant is judged on the facts as they appeared to her. If information does not on those facts have the appearance of being confidential, she is not required to carry out inquiries to resolve possible doubts.[30] That there might be some question is not sufficient.[31] But if, on those facts, a reasonable person would have appreciated that the information *is* confidential, then the defendant will owe a duty of confidence, whether or not she subjectively appreciates that fact. The doctrine of constructive notice, in other words, must be applied. But it must be applied sensibly and with regard to its context. A solicitor who receives documents from a professional opponent, for instance, will normally be entitled to assume that disclosure was deliberate, not mistaken; only if error is 'obvious' will any obligation be imposed. A litigant in person might be held to an even less stringent standard. Thus a realistic and practical view will be taken of what the defendant ought to appreciate; but the test will remain objective.

TIME AT WHICH NOTICE IS RELEVANT

In principle, the question whether the defendant has notice that information is confidential is to be tested at the date when the act complained of takes place—that is, when the information in question is used or disclosed—and not at the date of its acquisition. Thus if a defendant receives information in innocent good faith, but subsequently learns that it is confidential, a duty of confidence is owed:

> [H]owever innocent the acquisition of the knowledge, what will be restrained is the use or disclosure of it after notice of the impropriety.[32]

[28] [2000] FSR 718.

[29] Though there was authority bearing on the question (see nn 6 and 18 above) which was not considered.

[30] See, in particular, the approach taken to the cases of mistaken disclosure of privileged documents, p 27 above.

[31] Thus knowledge that confidence is asserted is not enough: *Fraser v Thames Television Ltd* [1984] QB 44, 65 (Hirst J).

[32] *Malone v Metropolitan Police Commissioner* [1979] Ch 344, 361 (Megarry V-C). See also *Fraser v Evans* [1969] QB 349 (CA), 361 (Lord Denning MR); *Surface Technology plc v Young* [2002] FSR 25, [27] (Pumfrey J).

This is as it should be. For a person who acquires information innocently but then realises it is confidential ought not to be allowed to disregard this later, and better, knowledge based upon earlier ignorance. It is, however, conceivable that a person who has acquired information in good faith may have a defence in certain circumstances if, after its acquisition, she has changed her position to her detriment in the mistaken belief that she is free to use the information—a point which might well be thought to alter the equities of the situation, and is considered in § 19, below.

§ 6

Misuse

Information is protected against misuse by a defendant. Misuse consists of any use of protected information (including use by disclosure) whose purpose, manner or extent violates the claimant's reasonable expectations which the defendant has agreed to respect or of which the defendant has notice.

MOST CASES OF breach of confidence involve *disclosure* of information in a way that violates the claimant's reasonable expectation of confidentiality. In a simple case that is all that matters: the claimant expects the information to be kept secret (from everyone), and the defendant is obliged to keep the information secret (from everyone).

But the position is not always so simple. On the one hand, the defendant may make use of confidential information which does not involve its disclosure, for instance by using a confidential formula to manufacture a drug, or using a confidential customer-list to contact customers. It is well-established that such activities may involve a breach of confidence: the duty is 'not merely not to communicate the information to a third party', but 'not . . . to make any use of it or cause any use to be made of it by others',[1] or not to use it except for some limited purpose.[2]

On the other hand, not *all* disclosure of confidential information will constitute misuse. Quite apart from limitations such as those permitting disclosure in the public interest (which are discussed in Part II), there may be many cases where disclosure does not amount to misuse. For instance, a lawyer engaged in litigation may disclose confidential information to witnesses or experts for the purposes of the litigation. Or a doctor might disclose medical information to a consultant to enable treatment to take place.

Those are simple cases, in which the claimant may be taken to have expressly or impliedly consented to the relevant disclosure. But there are other, less simple, cases. Take, for example, sexual relationships. These are (now) classic instances of cases where confidentiality is assumed: 'when people kiss and later

[1] *Prince Jefri Bolkiah v KPMG* [1999] 2 AC 222 (HL), 235 (Lord Millett).

[2] *Smith Kline & French Laboratories (Australia) Ltd v Department of Community Services* [1990] FSR 617, 641 (Gummow J).

one of them tells, that second person is almost certainly breaking a confidential relationship'.[3] But it would be wrong to regard the confidence as absolute. It is likely to extend to some aspects of the relationship but not others (for instance, not always the fact of the relationship, as opposed to its details[4]). It also seems likely that a nuanced approach might also have to be taken to different sorts of disclosure. Lovers and spouses may have a reasonable expectation that the details of their relationship will not be published to the world, but it might not be reasonable to expect each to keep the details secret from close friends, religious counsellors, or professional advisers. It is improbable that a person who confesses adultery to his priest, or talks about an affair with her psychoanalyst, commits any breach of confidence.

How, then, is the question of misuse to be judged? The answer is that in applying the tests set out in §§ 2, 4 and 5 the court does not merely look to see whether the information is confidential or not—a question admitting of a simple answer 'yes' or 'no'—but explores the reasonable expectation of the claimant, and the defendant's position with respect to it, in more depth. The court seeks to ascertain what restrictions on the use of information the claimant can reasonably expect, and how far the defendant has agreed to or has notice of those restrictions. The court must also establish the facts about the defendant's conduct. Particularly in cases of alleged misuse other than by disclosure, the claimant is expected to establish (directly or as a matter of inference) what use has been made of the information.[5] The court then asks whether the obligation of confidence has been 'abused', whether unconscientious use has been made of the information, looking at that question from the perspective of the person of 'average intelligence and honesty',[6] and asking whether such a person's conscience would be troubled by the proposed use (including use by disclosure) of the confidential information.[7] All these tests involve looking at the matter objectively. Misuse need not be deliberate, or done with any consciousness of wrongdoing. The question is whether the defendant's conscience *ought* to be troubled—not whether it actually is.

[3] *Barrymore v News Group Newspapers Ltd* [1997] FSR 600, 603 (Jacob J).

[4] *Ibid*, but contrast *Lord Browne of Madingley v Associated Newspapers Ltd* [2007] EWCA Civ 295, [2007] 3 WLR 289, [61].

[5] *Arklow Investments Ltd v Maclean* [2000] 1 WLR 594 (PC), 601–2 (Henry J). It was there held that the mere fact that a person had been 'galvanised' into action by confidential information did not amount to misuse.

[6] *Printers & Finishers Ltd v Holloway* [1965] RPC 239, 257 (Cross J).

[7] *R v Department of Health, ex parte Source Informatics Ltd* [2001] QB 424 (CA), [24] (Simon Brown LJ).

Part II

Limiting Principles

§7

Loss of Confidentiality

Information will not be protected where it has become so generally accessible that, in all the circumstances, it can no longer be regarded as confidential.

THE GENERAL PRINCIPLE

WHERE INFORMATION IS freely available, it is no longer protected, even if the defendant originally acquired it in confidence. The general principle, which is subject to a number of qualifications (they are not genuinely exceptions) is well-established. Thus in a leading case, *O Mustad & Son v Dosen*,[1] the confidential information had been published by being included in a patent application: it could therefore no longer be protected. The law of confidentiality does not protect information that is 'public property and public knowledge.'[2] The vitality of the general principle was confirmed in *Spycatcher*.[3] It was not doubted by any member of the House of Lords in *Douglas v Hello! (No 3)*[4] although there was disagreement as to its application). It is therefore necessary to explore the extent of the principle.

FREE AVAILABILITY

There seems, at least as a matter of first impression, to be some inconsistency between the cases. Sometimes, the courts seem to ask themselves the question: *could* a person who wished to do so find this information out (in some way) from non-confidential sources? Is the information *available*, albeit with difficulty? No doubt few members of the public knew about Mustad's special process for making fish-hooks.[5] But any interested person (including the defendant) could have found it out: so the process was not confidential. Courts

[1] (1928), *Note* [1964] 1 WLR 109 (HL).

[2] *Saltman Engineering Co Ltd v Campbell Engineering Co Ltd* (1948) 65 RPC 203 (CA), 215 (Lord Greene MR).

[3] *Attorney-General v Guardian Newspapers Ltd* (No 2) [1990] 1 AC 109 (HL), 282.

[4] [2007] UKHL 21, [2007] 2 WLR 920.

[5] *Mustad v Dosen* [1964] 1 WLR 109 (HL).

have held that criminal convictions—since they are matters of 'public record'—are not capable of being confidential.[6] So too, once a document is referred to in open court it may lose its confidential status.[7] It has (at least in the past) sometimes been held that something that occurred 'in public', observable to anyone who happened to be present, could not be confidential.[8] Such cases seem to be applying an abstract test of whether the information is 'capable of being discovered' (or, perhaps, was ever capable of being discovered) by the public.

Yet other cases take a more protective approach. That is certainly true today with regard to events 'observable to' the public.[9] But it is true more generally. Thus as long ago as 1897, it was held that the fact that the results of horse races were known to race-goers where they took place did not preclude confidentiality in that information when transmitted to subscribers at some distance from the race. It had not been published so as to be 'made known to the whole world'.[10] Obviously confidentiality is 'not defeated simply by proving that there are other people in the world who know the facts in question'.[11] Even where the information has been published in the media, protection will not necessarily be lost.[12] Thus, in *Spycatcher*, although holding that confidentiality had in the circumstances of that case been lost, Lord Keith explained that an individual whose private affairs were published in a newspaper in one country might still be able to prevent republication on a wider basis elsewhere.[13] And in another case[14] Butler-Sloss P declined to accept that information was not confidential just because it could be pieced together by dint of research in libraries and statistical publications. Cases such as these suggest that the true test is not so much whether the information is 'available' as whether it is already so widely known that further protection will serve no purpose at all.[15]

How is one to reconcile these approaches? The answer, it is suggested, is that the question is one of 'degree depending on the particular case'.[16] The key deter-

[6] *Hilton v Barker Booth & Eastwood* [2005] UKHL 8, [2005] 1 WLR 567, [7] (Lord Scott); *Elliott v Chief Constable of Wiltshire, The Times*, 5 Dec 1996.

[7] *Long Beach Ltd v Global Witness Ltd* [2007] EWHC 1980 (QB), applying the same principle to disclosure in open court in Hong Kong.

[8] *Woodward v Hutchins* [1977] 1 WLR 760 (CA).

[9] See above, p 10.

[10] *Exchange Telegraph Co Ltd v Central News Ltd* [1897] 2 Ch 48, 53 (Stirling J).

[11] *Franchi v Franchi* [1967] RPC 149, 152 (Cross J). See also *Stephens v Avery* [1988] Ch 449, 554 (Browne-Wilkinson V-C).

[12] *Schering Chemicals Ltd v Falkman Ltd* [1982] QB 1 (CA); *Creation Records Ltd v News Group Newspapers Ltd* [1997] EMLR 44; *Mills v News Group Newspapers Ltd* [2001] EMLR 41, [25] (Lawrence Collins J); *Gilbert v Star Newspapers Ltd* (1994) 11 TLR 4.

[13] [1990] 1 AC 109, 260.

[14] *Attorney-General v Greater Manchester Newspapers Ltd, The Times*, 7 Dec 2001.

[15] But compare the approach of Stanley Burnton J in *Long Beach Ltd v Global Witness Ltd* [2007] EWHC 1980 (QB), [41]–[44] in relation to publication on the internet. It is open to question whether that approach is wholly consistent with the authorities referred to above.

[16] *Franchi v Franchi* [1967] RPC 149, 153 (Cross J). See also *Northern Rock plc v The Financial Times Ltd* [2007] EWHC 2677 (QB), [15] (Tugendhat J): 'Whether or not the fact that information has become available to the public should lead to a refusal of an injunction requires a qualitative and not just a quantitative assessment'.

mining factors are the type of information (and nature of the confidentiality interest), and the nature of the likely 'audience' for it. If the question relates to the disclosure of information to the general public, then only quite widespread publication will result in the loss of confidentiality. The general public is not expected to spend its time searching specialised archives and statistical data, so that even republication may well amount to a breach of confidence. That is perhaps especially true where the information is personally sensitive, engaging privacy interests.[17] On the other hand, if information is really 'of interest' to a specialised group of people—such as foreign intelligence agencies or trade competitors—who can be expected to pursue it vigorously even in obscure places, much less extensive publication will be enough to destroy confidentiality. The *test* being applied in each case is the same: is the information 'so generally accessible that, in all the circumstances, it can no longer be regarded as confidential'.[18] But the application of the test depends on the particular circumstances of the case.

Particular attention must also be paid to the exact nature of the information. The fact that a written account of an event is publicly available does not mean that photographs of that event will not remain confidential. Indeed, the fact that some photographs have been published does not necessarily mean that other photographs (even if they show the same event) may not be confidential, since the exact image makes a difference.[19] Similarly, the fact that a boy named Venables was convicted of murder may be a matter of public record; but the fact that X (now known under a different name) is that boy is not.[20] A compilation of publicly available information may convey new information which is not regarded as publicly available, even if the individual pieces of it are.[21]

The fact that information is not protected as confidential does not, of course, mean that it may not be protected in some other way. A contract or professional engagement may impose obligations not to disclose information which the law of confidentiality, as such, would not protect.[22] So too may public law.[23] But the duty of confidence, as such, does not apply once information is published.

THE IDENTITY OF THE PUBLISHER

It was at one time believed that the principle set out in § 7 applied only where the *claimant* was responsible for the publication (as had in fact been the case in

[17] *McKennitt v Ash* [2005] EWHC (QB), [2006] EMLR 10, [81] (Eady J); *W B v H Bauer Publishing Ltd* [2002] EMLR 8, [26] (Eady J).

[18] *Attorney-General v Guardian Newspapers Ltd* (*No 2*) [1990] 1 AC 109, 282 (Lord Goff). This was the test applied by Eady J in *McKennitt v Ash* [2005] EWHC 3003 (QB), [2006] EMLR 10, [81].

[19] Thus the majority in *Douglas v Hello! Ltd* (*No 3*) [2007] UKHL 21, [2007] 2 WLR 920.

[20] *Venables v News Group Newspapers Ltd* [2001] Fam 430.

[21] See *R v Chief Constable of North Wales Police, ex parte Thorpe* [1999] QB 396, 415 (Buxton J).

[22] *Hilton v Barker Booth & Eastwood* [2005] UKHL 8, [2005] 1 WLR 567.

[23] *R v Chief Constable of North Wales Police, ex parte Thorpe* [1999] QB 396 (CA).

Mustad[24]). In effect it was treated as a form of waiver by consent. It followed that it was not applied where the publication had been carried out by the *defendant*, in breach of his duty of confidence,[25] or where it had been carried out by a third party.[26]

It seems, since *Spycatcher*,[27] that the distinctions between 'authorised' and 'unauthorised' publication are not sound. The only question is whether confidentiality has been lost; it does not matter how it has been lost.[28] The duty of confidence ends once the information comes into the public domain, however that happens. That principle, however, does not have such far-reaching consequences as might at first appear, for a variety of reasons.

First, so far as remedies in the form of damages or an account of profits are concerned, liability will not end at the point where the information first becomes public. If the defendant is liable for publishing confidential information which is confidential when it is first published, he will be liable for all the loss caused (or all the profit made) by that breach. This may include losses suffered by the claimant after the initial publication. Indeed, it may extend to losses which are suffered because third parties are encouraged, as a result of the defendant's breach, themselves to publish or re-publish the information.[29] Subsequent republication may not involve any further breach of duty, but in so far as it is made possible by the initial breach, the loss flowing from it remains recoverable. The same principle applies to an account of profits: if *D* publishes information—thereby destroying its confidentiality—and then republishes it later, the second publication is not itself a breach of confidence. But the profits made from the second publication are still caused by the original breach—but for which the second publication could have been enjoined—and *D* is therefore accountable for the entire profit from both publications.

Secondly, the position may be different where there is a contract, because the parties may by contract agree not to use or publish information even if that information is not confidential. In those circumstances publication even of information that is no longer confidential may be a breach of contract entitling the innocent party to damages or (in an appropriate case) to an account of profits.[30]

[24] [1964] 1 WLR 109 (HL).

[25] *Speed Seal Products Ltd v Paddington* [1985] 1 WLR 1327 (CA).

[26] *Cranleigh Precision Engineering Ltd v Bryant* [1965] 1 WLR 1293.

[27] *Attorney-General v Guardian Newspapers* (*No 2*) [1990] 1 AC 109 (HL). On this point Lord Keith (at 259), Lord Brightman (at 266), and Lord Goff (at 289), all seem to have regarded the duty of confidence, as such, as ended by the publication, unauthorised though it was. Lord Griffiths disagreed. Lord Jauncey's position is unclear.

[28] Toulson & Phipps, paras 4–015 to 4–016, take the same view. In *EPI Environmental Technologies Inc v Symphony Plastic Technologies plc* [2006] EWCA Civ 3, [49], Jacob LJ suggested that it might make a difference whether it was the claimant who puts the information in the public domain, but his remarks were clearly *obiter*.

[29] See *Douglas v Hello! Ltd* (*No 7*) [2003] EWHC 2629 (Ch), [2004] EMLR 2, affirmed on this point [2007] UKHL 21, [2007] 2 WLR 920.

[30] See, eg, *Attorney-General v Blake*, [2001] 1 AC 268 (HL).

SPRINGBOARD INJUNCTIONS

One apparent exception to § 7 deserves special consideration. Where a defendant has obtained confidential information from the claimant, he may be restrained from using that information even though it would be possible for him to obtain the equivalent information from untainted sources. The essence of the doctrine was explained by Roxburgh J in *Terrapin Ltd v Builders Supply Co (Hayes) Ltd* using the language of the 'springboard' from which the injunction gets its name:

> [A] person who has obtained information in confidence is not allowed to use it as a spring-board for activities detrimental to the person who made the confidential communication, and spring-board it remains even when all the features have been published and can be ascertained.[31]

At first sight this is an exception to § 7, since the springboard injunction prevents the defendant from using information that is publicly and freely available. But on closer analysis, it is not. For in fact, the 'information' in question is these cases is *not* freely available. The information that is available may cover the same ground, and may be capable of being assembled into the same form, but the exact information is not available. Thus, as Roxburgh J pointed out in *Terrapin*, the information that was publicly available about the claimant's products (in the form of brochures and the products themselves) was not identical to the confidential plans and specifications. Or, as Lord Denning MR put it in *Seager v Copydex Ltd*[32] the information is 'partly public and partly private'. In principle the private information remains private. But it is possible to use the public information to *recreate* the private information. The only difficulty is to fashion a remedy which protects that private information without also (impermissibly) giving protection in respect of public information. The springboard injunction aims to achieve that result, effectively putting the defendant in the same position he would be in—neither better nor worse—if he scrupulously avoided making any use of the private information, which remains protected, and instead took the time and trouble needed to recreate the private information from scratch based on the public information. So understood, the springboard cases are not true exceptions to § 7.

The purpose of the injunction, then, is to prevent the defendant from enjoying the unfair advantage which might be expected to accrue from the misuse of *confidential* information, while preserving the defendant's right to use non-confidential information. It must not therefore extend beyond the period of time for which that advantage can be expected to accrue.[33] To restrain the defendant completely and permanently would be to give undue weight to the claimant's

[31] (1959), [1967] RPC 375, 391.
[32] [1967] 1 WLR 923 (CA), 931.
[33] *Roger Bullivant Ltd v Ellis* [1987] ICR 464 (CA), 476 (Neill LJ).

interests, ignoring the fact that the defendant could (with some trouble) obtain the information in such a way that he is free to use it. But not to restrain him at all would enable him to benefit, compared to the claimant and others, by his wrong.

The injunction is therefore granted where the claimant demonstrates (*a*) that the defendant is making unlawful use of confidential information, or threatens to do so, (*b*) that the defendant has thereby obtained a competitive advantage, and (*c*) that the advantage subsists at the date the injunction is granted and is likely to subsist for the duration of the injunction.[34]

[34] *Sun Valley Foods Ltd v Vincent* [2000] FSR 825, 834 (Jonathan Parker J).

§ 8

Trivial Information

Trivial information is not protected.

MANY STATEMENTS CAN be found in the cases to the effect that trivial information will not be protected (even if it is confidential). The principle was endorsed by Megarry J in *Coco v Clark*[1] and by Lord Goff in *Spycatcher*.[2] It was referred to with approval by Lord Walker in *Douglas v Hello! Ltd*.[3]

In theory this is so, and it is possible to think of hypothetical examples, such as disclosing plans for a surprise party to a friend. In practice it is hard to find convincing examples of cases which fail on this ground.[4] Even celebrities rarely litigate over the genuinely trivial. The argument deployed in *Stephens v Avery*[5] that sexual relationships between non-married persons were unworthy of protection was rejected then, and would now be decisively rejected. Quite the contrary:

> the argument that information is trivial or anodyne carries much less weight in a case concerned with facts about an individual's private life which he or she reasonably expects to be confidential.[6]

Sexual relationships are now regarded as a paradigm case where information is likely to be protected. Phillipson[7] makes the valuable point that there is a danger of confusing information that is trivial from the point of view of the public interest in communicating it with information that is trivial in the sense

[1] *Coco v A N Clark (Engineers) Ltd* [1969] RPC 41, 48: 'equity ought not to be invoked merely to protect tittle-tattle, however confidential'.

[2] *Attorney-General v Guardian Newspapers Ltd (No 2)* [1990] 1 AC 109 (HL), 282: 'the duty of confidence applies neither to useless information, nor to trivia'.

[3] [2007] UKHL 21, [291]: 'the law of confidence does not protect trivia'.

[4] For a rare possible example see *McNicol v Sportsman's Book Stores* (1930) [1928–35] *MacGillivray's Copyright Cases* 116. In *McKennitt v Ash* [2005] EWHC 3003 (QB), [2006] EMLR 10, [139] protection was refused for information about a shopping trip, which was 'trivial and of no consequence', although other information was protected.

[5] [1988] Ch 449.

[6] *Douglas v Hello! Ltd (No 3)* [2007] UKHL 21, [2007] 2 WLR 920, [291] (Lord Walker).

[7] G Phillipson, 'Transforming Breach of Confidence? Towards a Common Law Right of Privacy under the Human Rights Act' (2003) *MLR* 726, 757.

of unimportant to the individual concerned. Information about sexual and intimate relationships is frequently trivial from the first perspective (there is little public interest in knowing such information), yet often extremely significant for the individual concerned.

In the commercial sphere, too, protection does not depend on showing that the information is of public importance. Seemingly unspectacular information, such as pictures destined for an album-cover,[8] the plot of a play,[9] or the appearance of a bride at her wedding[10] may all be protected.

In practice 'triviality' is unlikely to be important as a complete defence. It is more likely to be a factor that is brought into account in deciding whether information is confidential or in deciding whether the right to freedom of expression or the public interest permit disclosure of otherwise confidential information.[11]

[8] *Creation Records Ltd v News Group Newspapers Ltd* [1997] EMLR 444.

[9] *Gilbert v Star Newspaper Co Ltd* (1894) 11 TLR 4.

[10] *Douglas v Hello! Ltd* (*No 3*) [2007] UKHL 21, [2007] 2 WLR 920.

[11] See, for instance, *Mills v News Group Newspapers Ltd* [2001] EMLR 41, and §§ 11 and 17, below.

§ 9

Disclosure Required by Law

Information is not protected if its disclosure or use is required by law.

ALL COMMON LAW obligations of confidence necessarily give way to any statutory rule compelling disclosure.[1] That is true even of express contractual obligations: an express obligation to conceal information that statute requires to be disclosed is void.[2] Little further commentary is required on the basic principle. Thus, a party to litigation who is required to disclose documents cannot refuse to do so because they are confidential, and breaches no duty in doing so.[3] A third party required to produce documents, pursuant to a statutory power, cannot refuse to do so on the grounds that the information sought is confidential, and breaches no duty in doing so.[4] It is not a breach of confidence for a witness who is compelled to give evidence to do so.[5] To qualify under this principle, however, the disclosure must be required by the law applicable to the confidentiality obligations. Where those are governed by English law—as for example where a bank account is subject to English law[6]—the fact that a foreign court orders disclosure will not be sufficient justification in itself.[7]

[1] *Tournier v National Provincial and Union Bank of England* [1924] 1 KB 461 (CA), 473, in which Bankes LJ took disclosure 'under compulsion of law' as his first example of how the duty of confidence is qualified; *Parry-Jones v Law Society* [1969] 1 Ch 1 (CA), 9 (Diplock LJ).

[2] *Parry-Jones v Law Society* [1969] 1 Ch 1, 9 (Diplock LJ).

[3] *Science Research Council v Nassé* [1980] AC 1028 (HL); *Alfred Crompton Amusement Machines Ltd v Commissioners of Customs and Excise (No 2)* [1974] AC 405 (HL).

[4] For instance the Banker's Books Evidence Act 1879: see *Tournier v National Provincial and Union Bank of England* [1924] 1 KB 461, 473 (Bankes LJ).

[5] *Robertson v Canadian Imperial Bank of Commerce* [1994] 1 WLR 1493 (PC); *Barclays Bank plc v Taylor* [1989] 1 WLR 1066 (CA).

[6] It is simple enough to identify the applicable law where the confidentiality arises from a contract. Where confidentiality is non-contractual, the position with regard to the applicable law is obscure. It is suggested that it is *probably* the law of the country in which the events occur or (if that is inappropriate or there is more than one such country) the law of the country with which the alleged breach is most closely connected, ie, in effect, and perhaps in strict theory, the rule applicable to torts under Part III of the Private International Law (Miscellaneous Provisions) Act 1995.

[7] *X AG v A Bank* [1983] 2 All ER 464. But disclosure may be permissible if the interests of justice require it: see §14 and, eg, *Pharaon v Bank of Credit and Commerce International SA* [1998] 4 All ER 455. The appropriate course is to apply for an order from the English court under letters of request.

The reach of this rule, however, depends on the breadth of the obligation to disclose. That must always turn on two questions: (*a*) the construction of the rule, and in particular whether it requires *confidential* information to be disclosed, or empowers a court or other person to require confidential information to be disclosed; and (*b*), to the extent that the rule confers a discretion, the exercise of that discretion. Confidentiality may be a relevant factor in both inquiries.

Statutory duties to disclose information, or powers to require its disclosure, may contain express exceptions for confidential information. Thus, for instance, the Freedom of Information Act 2000 contains various relevant exemptions[8] which prevent public authorities from being obliged to disclose confidential information. Apart from these express exceptions, there is a presumption against interpreting statutes as imposing a duty to disclose, or conferring a power to require disclosure of confidential information that is subject to legal professional privilege.[9] Thus, for instance, a court has no power to order disclosure of a privileged document or compel a witness to reveal privileged information. This is not a matter of discretion, but of right.[10] Under section 3 of the Human Rights Act 1998, a similar approach ought to be taken to any statutory provision that is or could be incompatible with rights under Article 8 of the Convention.[11]

So far as discretion is concerned, even where there is a power to order disclosure of confidential information, it is well-established that confidentiality will be a relevant consideration in exercising the discretion. The court will therefore take account of confidentiality in deciding whether a document should be disclosed,[12] or a witness compelled to produce a document or answer a question which would involve revealing confidential information.[13] In *Attorney-General v Mulholland*[14] Lord Denning MR, after noting the special position of lawyers, explained:

> Take the clergyman, the banker or the medical man. None of these is entitled to refuse to answer when directed to by a judge. Let me not be mistaken. The judge will respect the confidences which each member of these honourable professions receives in the course of it, and will not direct him to answer unless not only it is relevant but also it

[8] See, in particular, s 40 (personal information), s 42 (legal professional privilege), s 41 (information provided in confidence), and s 43 (trade secrets).

[9] *R (Morgan Grenfell Ltd) v Special Commissioner of Income Tax* [2002] UKHL 21, [2003] 1 AC 563; *Bowman v Fels* [2005] EWCA Civ 225, [2005] 1 WLR 3083, [85]–[91]; *General Mediterranean Holdings SA v Patel* [2000] 1 WLR 272, 295 (Toulson J).

[10] *R v Derby Magistrates Court, ex parte B* [1996] 1 AC 487 (HL).

[11] Note also the common law presumption that fundamental rights are not overridden by general words: *R v Secretary of State for the Home Department, ex parte Simms* [2000] 2 AC 115 (HL); *Bowman v Fels* [2005] EWCA Civ 225, [2005] 1 WLR 3083, [81]–[82].

[12] *Science Research Council v Nassé* [1980] AC 1028 (HL).

[13] See, eg, *Hassneh Insurance Co of Israel v Mew* [1993] 2 Lloyd's Rep 243, 250–1 (Colman J). The principle also applies where the witness is asked questions concerning information private to himself: *Morgan v Morgan* [1977] Fam 122.

[14] [1963] 2 QB 477 (CA).

> is a proper and, indeed, necessary question in the course of justice to be put and answered.[15]

Similar principles ought to guide any decision-maker exercising a statutory power to require information to be provided. To the extent that the privacy interests concerned engage Article 8 of the Convention, the discretion must be exercised in a way compatible with the Convention.[16]

[15] *Ibid*, 489.

[16] Human Rights Act 1998, s 6.

§ 10

Disclosure with Consent

Information is not to be protected from disclosure or use to which the claimant has expressly or impliedly consented.

THE BASIC PRINCIPLE is not in doubt: one cannot as a matter of good sense and justice complain of being wronged by an act to which one consented.[1] Thus it is clearly a defence to an action for breach of confidence to show that the claimant consented to the disclosure.[2] But, as with other areas of the law, the application of the maxim (and particularly keeping it in proper bounds) is more troublesome.

CONSENT: VARIOUS USES

Appeals to 'consent' occur in various different senses or contexts, which need to be kept distinct. In the first place, since the very existence and extent of an obligation of confidence depends on the expectations of the parties, 'consent' broadly understood is relevant to the questions whether there is any duty of confidence at all (in other words, the matters addressed in §§ 2, 4 and 5). It sometimes seems natural to say, when asking whether a claimant had a reasonable expectation of confidentiality in particular circumstances, that she 'must have consented' or 'impliedly consented' to a particular use of information. This is really just one way of expressing the conclusion that the claimant's reasonable expectations did not extend to preventing such-and-such a use of information, having regard to all the circumstances. There is nothing wrong with such usage, but it is convenient to distinguish the slightly different case where a person who *does* have such expectations, and *is* owed a duty of confidentiality, decides to release the person who owes that obligation from it after it has arisen. This is, however, a matter only of clarity of analysis and exposition: the underlying principle is the

[1] See Tugendhat & Christie para 9.08, citing *Smith v Baker & Sons* [1890] AC 323 (HL), 360 (Lord Herschell), where the general principle is stated.

[2] *Tournier v National Provincial and Union Bank of England* [1924] 1 KB 461 (CA), 473 (Bankes LJ).

same in both cases. The claimant's rights depend upon *unauthorised* use of confidential information, in a way that defeats the claimant's reasonable expectations.

A second category of case is more troublesome, for it involves the use of 'consent' and related concepts such as 'waiver' in an extended or even fictitious sense. Courts sometimes identify consent (particularly 'implied' consent) in circumstances where what really seems to be happening is some balancing of the public interest in disclosure which has nothing to do with consent at all. Thus, for instance, it is long-established that a person entitled to legal professional privilege may waive that privilege, by consenting to the information being used or made public. No difficulty arises with express waiver; that is consent pure and simple. But there are also categories of 'implied waiver' which seem to rest more on public policy grounds than on any true understanding of consent.

For instance, those who sue their solicitors impliedly waive privilege in the confidential information concerning the relationship.[3] And a person who deploys part of a privileged document in court impliedly waives privilege in the whole of that document, and in other documents dealing with the 'whole of the issue in question'[4] or the same 'transaction'.[5] Although described as cases of 'waiver' (in those cases not just of confidentiality but of privilege) such instances do not depend on any voluntary decision by the claimant to permit disclosure or use. They rest, rather, on basic principles of fairness. A party cannot be permitted to sue his lawyers without allowing them to use material they already know about to defend themselves. And so, although it is said that the client bringing litigation against a solicitor 'releases the solicitor to that extent from the obligation of confidence by which he was formerly bound',[6] this is an 'implication of law',[7] whose rationale is to avoid unfairness and not a genuine attempt to identify implied consent in fact. A person could not avoid the implication by beginning proceedings while making it clear that no waiver of privilege is intended. So too with the principle against partial waiver: a party 'may not waive privilege in such a partial and selective manner that unfairness or misunderstanding may result'.[8] That remains the rule however strongly the waiving party may wish to be selective or partial, and even if that subjective desire is made explicitly clear. These rules, though collected under the rubric of 'waiver' and sometimes described as cases of 'implied waiver' are better regarded as

[3] See *Paragon Finance plc v Freshfields* [1999] 1 WLR 1183 (CA). The 'waiver' extends only to the material confidential to the lawyer sued, and not to other material.

[4] *Nea Karteria Maritime Co v Atlantic and Great Lakes Steamship Corp* [1981] Com LR 138, 139 (Mustill J).

[5] *General Accident Fire and Life Assurance Corp Ltd v Tanter* [1984] 1 WLR 100, 115 (Hobhouse J).

[6] *Paragon Finance Ltd v Freshfields* [1999] 1 WLR 1183 (CA), 1188 (Lord Bingham CJ).

[7] *Ibid.*

[8] *Ibid.* See also *General Accident Fire and Life Assurance Corp Ltd v Tanter* [1984] 1 WLR 100, 114 (Hobhouse J).

involving the application of the public policy that justice should be fairly administered (see § 14) and not on consent in any real sense.

The consent addressed in § 10 is voluntary permission given by the claimant to the defendant permitting use or disclosure of information which, when the permission is given, is subject to a duty of confidence. It is only in this narrow sense that it is necessary or desirable to refer to consent as in any sense an 'exception' or 'defence' to a breach of confidence claim.

WHAT CONSTITUTES CONSENT?

Consent may be express or implied.[9] In either case, the existence and ambit of consent is determined objectively, and not on the basis of either the claimant's or the defendant's subjective views. Thus in *Sunderland v Barclays Bank Ltd*[10] an account-holder discussing banking business on the telephone passed the receiver to her husband. It was held, applying an objective test, that she had impliedly consented to the bank discussing her affairs. The test applied was not what she believed, but what the bank manager 'justifiably' (that is, on an objective basis, reasonably) understood her to have consented to.[11]

Consent may also be a necessary implication from an act. For instance, if a customer asks a bank to provide a bank reference, she impliedly consents to the bank being released from its obligation to the extent necessary to provide the reference.[12] A patient who consents to be referred to a specialist impliedly consents to medical information being provided to the specialist.[13] But even here care must be taken as to the breadth of the consent. In *Cornelius v de Taranto*[14] the Court of Appeal held that consent to referral did not imply consent to the dissemination of a confidential report prepared for legal purposes, which went beyond the information reasonably required for treatment. As so often, all turns on the particular facts.[15]

Moreover, consent is not lightly to be implied. For instance, in *Attorney-General v Jonathan Cape Ltd*[16] it was suggested that since Richard Crossman's cabinet colleagues knew he kept a diary, they impliedly consented on behalf of the Crown to the publication of the information it contained. Lord Widgery CJ rejected that contention. Even if the other ministers had authority to consent, it

[9] *Tournier v National Provincial and Union Bank of England* [1924] 1 KB 461 (CA), 473 (Bankes LJ).

[10] (1938) 5 *Legal Decisions Affecting Bankers* 163.

[11] *Ibid*, 164 (Du Parcq LJ).

[12] *Turner v Royal Bank of Scotland plc* [1999] 2 All ER (Comm) 664 (CA). But there is no general implied consent permitting a bank to respond to 'status inquiries'.

[13] *Cornelius v de Taranto* [2001] EWCA Civ 1511, [2002] EMLR 6, [27] (Mantell LJ).

[14] [2001] EWCA Civ 1511, [2002] EMLR 6.

[15] Compare *Kapadia v London Borough of Lambeth* [2000] IRLR 699 (CA), [34] (Pill LJ), in which it was held that by consenting to be examined by a medical specialist on behalf of the opposing party to litigation, the patient impliedly consented to the disclosure of the report to that party.

[16] [1976] QB 752.

would have been necessary to show that they 'accepted [Crossman's] intention to use the diary whether it passed the scrutiny of the Cabinet Secretary or not'.[17] A few older cases[18] suggest that consent might be implied where the claimant has 'opened up' some area of private life to public speculation or comment. These should be regarded with considerable suspicion. As commentators have pointed out:

> the claim that previous, voluntary revelations constitute some sort of generalised all-purpose consent to future invasions of privacy is simply not plausible.[19]

'Consent' is invoked in these cases not because the court actually believes that the claimant is or ever was willing for the information to be used or published as it has been, but as:

> merely a cloak for a normative conclusion: that since in the past the plaintiff has sought publicity for personal information, she should not be allowed to complain about this publication.[20]

In other words, consent is used rather as 'waiver' is used in the 'implied waiver' cases described above.[21] This is merely confusing. That a claimant has 'opened up' his or her life previously to make it a matter of public comment, or publicly taken a stand on some issue, may be relevant as one of the factors in assessing whether publication is justified in order to safeguard freedom of expression (§ 17); but it does not indicate consent in any real sense.

Consent must, of course, be given by a person with the authority to consent, and with the capacity to do so.[22] There are occasional suggestions in the cases that it ought to be given in some particular form.[23] But those references seem to be dealing with what form it would have been prudent to use, rather than with any formal requirement. While it may be wise to obtain consent in writing or other permanent form, that is not required as a matter of law unless there is an express prior agreement to that effect.

[17] *Ibid*, 768 (Lord Widgery CJ).

[18] Notably *Woodward v Hutchins* [1977] 1 WLR 760 (CA) and *Lennon v News Group Ltd* [1978] FSR 575.

[19] G Phillipson and H Fenwick, 'Breach of Confidence as a Privacy Remedy in the Human Rights Act Era' (2000) 63 *MLR* 660, 680.

[20] *Ibid.*

[21] See p 50.

[22] *E v Channel Four Television* [2005] EWHC 1144, [2005] EMLR 30.

[23] *Cornelius v de Taranto* [2001] EWCA Civ 1511, [2002] EMLR 6, [27].

§ 11

Public Interest: Basic Principle

Information is not protected from disclosure that is required in the public interest.

THE GENERAL PRINCIPLE

IN *SPYCATCHER* LORD Goff identified a limitation on the protection offered by the common law as follows:

> [A]lthough the basis of the law's protection of confidence is that there is a public interest that confidences should be preserved and protected by the law, nevertheless that public interest may be outweighed by some other countervailing public interest which favours disclosure. This limitation may apply . . . to all types of confidential information. It is this limiting principle which may require a court to carry out a balancing operation, weighing the public interest in maintaining confidence against a countervailing public interest favouring disclosure.[1]

The principle developed out of and includes (but, as Lord Goff made clear, is not limited to) the principle that there is no confidence in 'iniquity'. It encompasses and reflects the notion that 'Danger to the State or public duty may supersede the duty' of confidant to confider.[2]

THE AMBIT AND SIGNIFICANCE OF THE PRINCIPLE

The case law exhibits a variety of opinion concerning the ambit and nature of the principle. Broadly, one may distinguish two incompatible approaches.

On one view, the principle is wide and directly applicable. It permits the court, in any case, to identify anything which might be described as *a* public interest in disclosure, and to set or weigh that against any interest in confidentiality. For example, in *Woodward v Hutchins*,[3] Lord Denning MR said, apparently in entirely general terms:

[1] *Attorney-General v Guardian Newspapers Ltd (No 2)* [1990] 1 AC 109 (HL), 282.
[2] *Weld-Blundell v Stephens* [1920] AC 956 (HL), 965 (Viscount Finlay).
[3] [1977] 1 WLR 760 (CA).

> In these cases of confidential information it is a case of balancing the public interest in maintaining the confidence against the public interest in knowing the truth.[4]

Toulson and Phipps rightly point out that such a broad statement—if read literally—invites the court to engage in an 'unstructured balancing exercise', assuming a 'general discretion whether or not to enforce confidentiality'.[5] It may become, as Gummow J put it:

> not so much a rule of law as an invitation to judicial idiosyncrasy by deciding each case on an ad hoc basis.[6]

The alternative view is that the principle expressed in § 11 constitutes a general principle, but one which is mediated through more specific principles whereby a particular (and important) public interest is identified, and obligations of confidentiality give way where the pursuit of that particular interest requires it. The balancing exercise is not general and unstructured, but specific and structured appropriately to the particular public interest in question. In many frequently occurring cases, its application can even be 'hardened' into specific rules that deal appropriately with the particular situation. Yet the categories of public interest are not closed (and to that extent the general principle remains important, not just as an organising principle), and they are not to be interpreted excessively narrowly—but by reference to the general principle. The general principle is still required because, as the Law Commission put it:

> [T]he range of circumstances in which the defence might properly be used is so wide and so variable that it is not practicable to define in general terms all the criteria to be used and that it would be misleading to single out particular issues . . . for consideration. . . . The public interest is a developing concept which changes with the social attitudes of the times.[7]

The defence therefore needs to be 'flexible enough to enable each case to be judged on its individual merits'.[8] But the flexibility comes not from applying a free-wheeling and unstructured balancing test in each case, but rather by recognising that accepted categories of the public interest are not rigidly fixed. They may require development, in the common-law fashion, incrementally and by analogy to respond to circumstances.

The second view is to be preferred. Apart from *Woodward*, the general approach taken in the cases has been to cleave closely to established categories

[4] *Ibid*, 764. See also *Dunford & Elliott Ltd v Johnson and Firth Brown Ltd* [1978] FSR 143 (CA), 148, where Lord Denning MR suggested that even an express obligation of confidentiality would not be enforced if it was, or had become, 'unreasonable'. A similar approach was suggested by Scott J in *Webster v James Chapman & Co* [1989] 3 All ER 939, 944–5, in which he said that 'protection is never given automatically', but always depends on a balance between the interests of the claimant in protection and those of the defendant in disclosure.

[5] Toulson & Phipps, para 6–017.

[6] *Smith Kline and French Laboratories (Australia) Ltd v Department of Community Services and Health* [1990] FSR 617, 663.

[7] Law Commission, *Working Paper on Breach of Confidence*, No 58 (1974), para 93.

[8] *Ibid*.

of the public interest. Moreover, as Lord Goff states the position, development inspired by the general principle does not merely involve balancing conflicting interests. Balancing is necessary, but before it takes place it is necessary to identify a specific countervailing public interest positively supporting disclosure. What is required is to weigh carefully all the relevant factors on both sides.[9]

DISCLOSURE ONLY TO THE EXTENT REQUIRED

The public interest defence does not generally operate in an 'all-or-nothing' way. It depends not only on identifying a public interest in disclosure, but a public interest in the sort of disclosure that the defendant has made or proposes to make. Thus, for instance, the public interest may justify disclosure to some appropriate authority, but it does not follow that general publication would be permissible.[10] Those cases where the defendant wishes to publish information generally are better handled under the principles applicable to freedom of expression (§ 17). They are better regarded as subject to a distinct principle, founded on respect for a constitutionally protected individual right, rather than as engaging simply an aspect of the public interest.

THE JURIDICAL BASIS OF THE PRINCIPLE

Although the existence of a public interest defence is not in doubt, there are five different, but overlapping, ways in which it can be analysed technically (not all of which will necessarily be available in any single case): (*a*) where there is a contract between the claimant and the defendant, as a principle employed in construing an express contractual obligation of confidentiality; (*b*) where there is a contract between the claimant and the defendant, as a principle employed in deciding whether an express contractual obligation of confidentiality is contrary to public policy; (*c*) where there is a contract between the claimant and the defendant, in deciding what terms are to be implied as to confidentiality; (*d*) where there is no contract between the claimant and the defendant, in deciding the extent to which the claimant has a *reasonable* expectation of confidentiality; (*e*) where the claimant seeks an equitable remedy, in deciding whether that remedy should as a matter of discretion be awarded, or in applying the maxim that the equitable claimant must have 'clean hands'.

[9] The guidelines developed by the courts for their own use in deciding whether to order disclosure to a third party of confidential material from proceedings involving children are useful as an example of the sort of factors that are relevant: see *Re C (A minor) (Care proceedings: Disclosure)* [1997] Fam 76 (CA), 85–6 (Swinton Thomas LJ).

[10] *W v Egdell* [1990] Ch 359, 389 (Scott J); *Attorney-General v Guardian Newspapers Ltd (No 2)* [1990] 1 AC 109 (HL), 269 (Lord Griffiths), 283 (Lord Goff); *Re A Company's Application* [1989] Ch 477, 481 (Scott J).

For the most part these differences of analysis do not produce any difference in outcome.[11] There seem to be three doubtful instances, where they might do so.

First, while it is undoubtedly the case that a term will not be implied which would have been contrary to public policy if it had been express,[12] implied obligations of confidentiality will not necessarily extend to everything that the parties might lawfully have provided for expressly. If that is so, then there is not complete symmetry between the scope of the public policy defence as it would apply in the face of an express term, and its scope where the terms are implied. If public policy would preclude enforcement of an express term, that is an end of the matter: no term will be implied.[13] But there may be a grey area, in relation to which the court would not hold that public policy so clearly required disclosure as to invalidate an express agreement to keep information confidential, but will not (on the other hand) imply a duty of confidentiality if none has been expressly provided.

In *Price Waterhouse v BCCI*,[14] for example, the court had to consider whether it was a breach of confidence for accountants to cooperate (voluntarily) with a non-statutory inquiry into the collapse of BCCI. Millett J held that, had there been an express agreement not to cooperate with the inquiry, it would not have been unenforceable as contrary to public policy.[15] But, nevertheless, he held that in the particular circumstances of the case, and in the absence of an express term dealing with the point, the public interest in favour of disclosure prevailed. In other words, he held that there is a 'grey area', where the court will enforce an express term but will not imply a term (or enforce a non-contractual equitable duty of confidence).

The decision has been criticised,[16] but is correct. It is a necessary condition before any term is implied that it should not be contrary to public policy. But it is not a sufficient condition. It is neither surprising nor contrary to principle that there may be cases where the parties are free to agree to treat information as confidential, but where in the absence of express agreement the court will not treat any such term as implied.[17] The test for public-interest disclosure where there is no express term is *not* limited to asking whether an express term purporting to preclude disclosure would be contrary to public policy.

Secondly, a related point has arisen in the authorities as to whether the existence of an express contractual term is relevant to the 'weight' to be attached to confidentiality when balancing it against some countervailing public interest.

[11] Toulson & Phipps, para 6–075: 'Where public interest is relied upon to justify disclosure . . . the courts have drawn no distinction between the position in equity and in contract.'

[12] *Initial Services Ltd v Putterill* [1968] 1 QB 396 (CA), 410 (Salmon LJ).

[13] *Ibid*; *Attorney-General v Guardian Newspapers Ltd* (No 2) [1990] 1 AC 109, 146 (Scott J).

[14] [1992] BCLC 583.

[15] *Ibid*, 601.

[16] See Toulson & Phipps, paras 6–043, 6–044.

[17] See also the discussion of express and implied terms in employment contracts at pp __ to __ below.

The authorities do not speak with one voice,[18] and the question has been left undecided by the Court of Appeal.[19] In principle, it is suggested, an express contractual term may be relevant at least as a factor demonstrating the importance attached by the parties to confidentiality. It is probably necessary to distinguish two situations. On the one hand, there are cases where confidentiality rests *solely* on agreement—the information would not normally be regarded as confidential, but the parties have agreed contractually to treat it as if it is. In those cases, the confidentiality interest will probably be regarded as relatively weak. On the other hand, there are cases where the information would be regarded as confidential even if there had not been any express agreement, *and* the parties have expressly so provided. In those cases, looking at the amalgam of circumstances through which a reasonable expectation of confidentiality is established, the express agreement tends to strengthen the force of the expectation. It operates synergistically with the other factors.

Thirdly, the 'clean hands' doctrine needs to be deployed with particular care. This maxim needs to be kept in check, because it could too easily become a vehicle for arbitrary ad hoc decisions based on broad sympathy for one party or the other. There is no doubt that it has from time to time been applied. But Spry's doubts appears justified, for the clean hands maxim is:

> often used in a purely rhetorical manner in cases where refusal of relief may better be justified on more precise grounds.[20]

Thus *Hubbard v Vosper*, in which the Court of Appeal denied relief to protect the course materials of the Church of Scientology was better decided on grounds that the public interest in freedom of expression justified publication to expose 'medical quackeries of a sort which may be dangerous if practiced behind closed doors'[21] than on the alternative ground that the claimants' methods of protecting their secrets were such that they did not come to the court with clean hands.[22]

A similar criticism applies to suggestions, such as those of Scott J in *Webster v James Chapman & Co*,[23] to the effect that the protection of confidential information always rests on the court's exercise of its equitable remedial discretion, and that the court may therefore always approach the matter in a highly flexible way, with an eye to the 'merits', broadly understood. This is a misunderstanding of the nature of the discretion involved. Although remedies for breach of confidence are often 'discretionary', the discretion is to be exercised in a predictable fashion to protect rights, not on ad hoc or idiosyncratic grounds.

[18] In *London Regional Transport v The Mayor of London* [2001] EWCA Civ 1491, [2003] EMLR 4, [46], Walker LJ expressed the view that no special weight was attributed to the existence of a contract. In *Attorney-General v Barker* [1990] 3 All ER 257 (CA), 260, Lord Donaldson MR said that it was.

[19] *Campbell v Frisbee* [2002] EWCA Civ 1374, [2003] ICR 141, [22].

[20] ICF Spry, *Equitable Remedies,* 7th edn (Pyrmont, 2001), 245.

[21] [1972] 2 QB 84, 96 (Lord Denning MR).

[22] *Ibid*, 101 (Megaw LJ).

[23] [1989] 3 All ER 939.

The 'clean hands' maxim, and the discretion to refuse relief, ought only to be applied circumspectly and in their proper sphere. The clean hands maxim:

> does not mean a general depravity; it must have an immediate and necessary relation to the equity sued for; it must be a depravity in a legal as well as in a moral sense.[24]

So applied, it bears little relation to the public interest defence in most cases. The discretion to refuse relief, also, is to be exercised on established principles, and not merely because the court would, in the particular case, prefer not to vindicate the claimant's rights. As Birks put it:

> [T]he advantages gained by certainty as to liability are nullified if the courts assert a free discretion as to remedy. The business of advising clients as to the advisability of litigation is rendered difficult by either form of uncertainty. It is hard to see remedial uncertainty as a lesser menace.[25]

THE INTERESTS RECOGNISED

A number of aspects of the public interest are so important or so frequently recognised in the cases that they deserve separate discussion: the detection, investigation and prevention of crime and serious wrongdoing (§ 12), public safety and health (§ 13), the administration of justice (§ 14), national security (§ 15), and the maintenance of reasonable competition (§ 16). Freedom of expression used to be a head of public interest, but is now better regarded as a free-standing principle (see § 17). It should not, however, be thought that these categories are rigid, or that they are comprehensive. Other interests may be recognised in an appropriate case. Thus, for instance, animal welfare has been recognised as a public interest.[26] So, although most cases arise under one of the well-established heads identified above, these should not be regarded as representing a closed or comprehensive class. The *basic* principle remains that set out in § 11.

RELATIONSHIP WITH ARTICLE 8 OF THE CONVENTION

In some cases in which breach of confidence is alleged, the claimant's rights concern private or family life, and are protected under Article 8 of the Convention. However Article 8 (2) permits interferences which are 'in accordance with law' and are

[24] *Dering v Earl of Winchelsea* (1787) 1 Cox 318, 319–20 (Eyre CB). See generally Meagher, Gummow & Lehane, paras 3–110, 3–130.

[25] P Birks, 'The Remedies for Abuse of Confidential Information' [1990] *LMCLQ* 460, 460–61.

[26] *Imutran Ltd v Uncaged Campaigns Ltd* [2001] 2 All ER 385.

> necessary in a democratic society in the interests of national security, public safety or the economic well-being of the country, for the prevention of disorder or crime, for the protection of health or morals, or for the protection of the rights and freedoms of others.

In general there seems little doubt that any interference caused by disclosure which is necessary for the public interest will meet these criteria. It will be 'in accordance with law' because it is well established, as a matter of law, that disclosure in the public interest is permissible. It will be necessary in a democratic society for one of the purposes set out in Article 8 (2) because the public interests recognised by the case law all correspond to matters identified in that paragraph, and because the test applied in each case is sufficiently stringent to satisfy the requirements of proportionality inherent in Article 8 (2). In effect, the court will have identified a 'pressing social need', for the interference, and weighed its proportionality having regard to the 'nature, context and importance of the right asserted and the extent of interference' balanced against 'the nature, context and importance of the public interest asserted as justification'.[27]

Accordingly, there is no need to construct separate rules to deal with cases in which claimants have Article 8 rights. That is not to say, of course, that the nature of those rights is not relevant to the inquiry, in the sense that wherever a balance falls to be struck between the public interest in confidentiality and the public interest in disclosure, the nature of the claimant's confidentiality interest is relevant. Interests protected under Article 8 naturally qualify for a high degree of protection.

[27] Lester and D Pannick (eds), *Human Rights Law and Practice,* 2nd edn (London, 2004), para 4.8.85.

§ 12

Public Interest: Wrongdoing

Information is not protected to the extent that the public interest in the detection, investigation and prevention of crime and serious wrongdoing outweighs the public interest in its confidentiality.

THE GENERAL POSITION

AN EARLY RECOGNITION of the public interest defence (though not under that name) was in *Gartside v Outram*,[1] in which a former employee defended himself against a claim by his former employers by alleging that they were involved in fraud on their principals. Sir William Page Wood V-C held that this was a potentially good defence:

> [T]here is no confidence as to the disclosure of iniquity. You cannot make me confidant of a crime or a fraud, and be entitled to close up my lips upon any secret which you have the audacity to disclose to me relating to any fraudulent intention on your part.[2]

At one time the principle was narrowly applied. For instance, in *Tournier*'s case, Bankes LJ thought that the banker's duty of confidence would not justify making disclosures to the police investigating crime.[3] In *Weld-Blundell v Stephens* he seemed to assume that the exception applied to anticipated or planned crimes, but not to past misdeeds. Where the wrong lay in the past, he suggested, 'public policy is better served by respecting the confidence than by abusing it'.[4]

Such a narrow view is no longer acceptable. The courts recognise a public interest in the detection as well as the prevention of crime,[5] in the provision of

[1] (1857) 26 LJ Ch (NS) 113.
[2] 26 LJ Ch (NS) 113, 114.
[3] [1924] 1 KB 461 (CA), 474.
[4] [1919] 1 KB 520 (CA), 527, aff'd [1920] AC 956 (HL).
[5] *Marlwood Commercial Inc v Kozeny* [2004] EWCA Civ 798, [2005] 1 WLR 104, [42]; *Initial Services Ltd v Putterill* [1968] 1 QB 396, 405 (Lord Denning MR).

information about non-criminal misdeeds to regulators,[6] in cooperation between English and foreign regulators,[7] and in cooperation by former auditors with a non-statutory inquiry into the affairs of a fraudulently run bank.[8] It could, in an appropriate case, justify the disclosure of past or anticipated civil wrongs to their victims.[9]

HOW THE BALANCE IS STRUCK

There is always *a* public interest in the detection and investigation of crime and wrongdoing. That public interest is strong, so that it will often outweigh the interest in confidentiality. But, as with any other public interest-based defence, there remains a balance to be struck. As Lord Denning MR put it, it is always 'essential' that the disclosure is 'justified in the public interest'.[10] What factors are to be considered?

The first factor is the strength of the public interest underlying confidentiality.[11] That is not the same in every case. For instance, although it is clear in general that the public interest may justify the disclosure of past as well as planned wrongdoing, that principle is not applied to confidences entrusted to lawyers—for there the public interest in allowing the client to be completely candid with a lawyer about the past is regarded as more important.[12] So if a lawyer, consulted after the commission of a crime for the purpose of being defended, threatened to disclose the client's confession to the prosecution, he could be restrained from doing so.[13] With lawyers, the line is drawn where the communication is made to the lawyer in furtherance of a current criminal plan, not where it merely discloses past wrongdoing.[14] (Though there is a shadowy area where the lawyer is engaged to 'cover up' a past fraud, rather than to advise about it.[15])

With doctors the distinction is drawn differently: doctors are justified in disclosing 'serious crime'.[16] The adjective, it is suggested, is important. There is a

[6] *Initial Services Ltd v Putterill* [1968] 1 QB 396 (CA) (breaches of the Restrictive Trade Practices Act 1956 to the Registrar); *Woolgar v Chief Constable of Sussex Police* [2000] 1 WLR 25 (CA) (disclosure to nursing regulator); *Re A Company's Application* [1989] Ch 477 (alleged breaches to financial services regulator and the Inland Revenue).

[7] *A v B Bank* [1993] QB 311.

[8] *Price Waterhouse v BCCI* [1992] BCLC 583.

[9] See *Gartside v Outram* (1857) 26 LJ Ch (NS) 113.

[10] *Initial Services Ltd v Putterill* [1968] 1 QB 396 (CA), 405.

[11] It is a fundamental error to regard the interest in confidence being maintained as merely a *private* interest of the claimant. It is a public interest: see *W v Egdell* [1990] Ch 359, 416 (Stephen Brown P). The nature and weight of the public interest in confidentiality varies.

[12] *R v Derby Magistrates Court, ex parte B* [1996] AC 487 (HL).

[13] *Weld-Blundell v Stephens* [1919] 1 KB 520 (CA), 544 (Scrutton LJ).

[14] *Bullivant v Attorney-General for Victoria* [1901] AC 195 (HL), 201 (Lord Halsbury); *O'Rourke v Darbishire* [1920] AC 581 (HL); *R v Cox* (1884) 14 QBD 153; *Butler v Board of Trade* [1971] Ch 68 (Goff J).

[15] See *Finers v Miro* [1991] 1 WLR 35 (CA), 40–41 (Dillon LJ).

[16] Advice from the General Medical Council, referred to with approval in *W v Egdell* [1990] Ch 359, 413 (Stephen Brown P), 421 (Bingham LJ), was in terms of disclosure of a 'grave or serious crime'.

public interest in patients being confident in disclosing to their doctors many things which might suggest some degree of criminal conduct. That suggests that it is by no means every confession of crime that the doctor ought to be free to disclose. A line has to be drawn however once the crimes involved are serious, especially where they are likely to cause serious harm to third parties.

The somewhat different obligations of lawyers and doctors represent a relatively well-explored example of a more general principle: the weight to be attached to obligations of confidence varies. And, as that weight varies, so the strength of the countervailing factors necessary to overcome the obligation varies.

The second factor is the strength of the public interest in the investigation or detection of the particular crime. At one end of the spectrum lie serious crimes or serious civil wrongs committed against third parties. It will only rarely be compatible with the public interest for a person to agree to conceal such a crime.[17] So, for instance, an agreement to prevent a person from giving evidence about serious wrongdoing to the police or third parties will be invalid as contrary to the public interest.[18] But it is dangerous to be too dogmatic, even in the case of quite serious crimes. A contract which relates only to volunteering evidence to the police about a fraud committed on a party may apparently be valid,[19] and (if valid) it is hard to see why it should not in an appropriate case be enforced. The rationale must be that the public interest in the investigation and prosecution of crime is not regarded as sufficient to outweigh the interest in the victim himself obtaining compensation, even by agreeing to keep information about the offence confidential. At the opposite end of the spectrum lie minor crimes or relatively trivial misdeeds. These are less likely to warrant disclosure.[20]

A third factor is the strength of the suspicions, and the nature of the information. There is an obvious difference between disclosing confidential information based on the merest suspicion or hint of wrongdoing, and disclosing such information where there is solid evidence of wrongdoing. In the context of lawyers, for instance, the courts permit disclosure only where there is a prima facie case that the information was communicated in furtherance of a criminal purpose.[21] The court has to walk a difficult line here. On the one hand, it cannot sensibly be expected to decide whether the suspicions are in fact justified—that is for the investigative body to which disclosure is made.[22] On the other hand, some assessment of the weight of the allegations to be made may be necessary. The mere assertion by the defendant that he has suspicions ought not to be enough.[23]

[17] Indeed, it will often be a criminal offence to do so: see Criminal Law Act 1967, s 5. S 5 implicitly accepts, however, that agreements for the concealment of some offences may be made.

[18] *Howard v Odhams Press Ltd* [1938] 1 KB 1 (CA).

[19] *Ibid*, 41 (Greene LJ).

[20] See the discussion of the duties of doctors, above.

[21] *Finers v Miro* [1991] 1 WLR 35, 40 (Dillon LJ).

[22] *Re A Company's Application* [1989] Ch 477, 483 (Scott J).

[23] In *Corrs Pavey Whiting & Byrne v Collector of Customs* (1987) 74 ALR 428, 450, Gummow J referred to communications whose subject matter was the 'existence *or real likelihood of the existence* of a . . . crime, civil wrong or serious misdeed of public importance'. In *Attorney-General v Guardian Newspapers (No 2)* [1990] 1 AC 109, 283, Lord Goff referred to allegations which

TO WHOM IS DISCLOSURE MADE?

In order to qualify under this head of the public interest, disclosure ought generally to be made to a regulatory or investigative body, such as the police, an appropriate regulator,[24] or public authority with a 'proper interest to receive the information'[25] or 'a real and direct interest in redressing such crime, wrong or misdeed'.[26] There may, however, be cases where disclosure to others is permissible, for instance if they are identified as potential victims of crime or wrongdoing, whom it is justifiable to warn.[27]

Some of authorities[28] suggest that in cases of serious wrongdoing disclosure to the public in general is justified. That is no doubt true. But, it is suggested, the public interest being pursued there is not so much that identified in § 12, the detection and prevention of crime, but rather the public interest in freedom of expression. That is not to say that such cases—dealing with the public *exposure* of disgraceful or criminal behaviour—are in any way wrongly decided, or that they do not reflect *a* public interest. But it seems better to regard the public interest in 'exposure' (for public comment, information, or censure) as different from the public interest in the communication of information which may lead to the detection or prevention, by the proper authorities, of crime or serious wrongdoing. Such disclosure by publication is best addressed through the principles set out in § 17.

'following such investigations as are reasonably open to the recipient, and having regard to all the circumstances of the case, . . . can reasonably be regarded as being a credible allegation from an apparently reliable source'.

[24] As in *Re A Company's Application* [1989] Ch 477 (financial services regulator and the Inland Revenue); *Francome v Mirror Group Newspapers Ltd* [1984] 1 WLR 892 (CA) (disclosure to jockey club and police).

[25] *Initial Services Ltd v Putterill* [1968] 1 QB 396 (CA), 406 (Lord Denning MR).

[26] *Corrs Pavey Whiting & Byrne v Collector of Customs* (1987) 74 ALR 428, 450 (Gummow J).

[27] See *Hellewell v Chief Constable of Derbyshire* [1995] 1 WLR 804 (Laws J) where the police were held justified in distributing photographs of known shoplifters to local traders. Laws J stressed that the dissemination 'was limited to parties having a reasonable concern to see it': [1995] 1 WLR 804, 811.

[28] *Initial Services Ltd v Putterill* [1968] 1 QB 396 (CA), 406 (Lord Denning MR); *Lion Laboratories Ltd v Evans* [1985] QB 526 (CA).

§ 13

Public Interest: Safety and Health

Information is not protected to the extent that the public interest in the protection of human life and health outweighs the public interest in its confidentiality.

THE INTERESTS RECOGNISED

THE COURTS NATURALLY recognise a public interest in the protection of human life and health (including psychological health)—'matters medically dangerous to the public'[1]—which may justify the disclosure of confidential information.

The recognition of this public interest is reflected in a number of cases (though often overlapping with the disclosure of information which would prevent crime). In *W v Egdell*[2] the claimant was a paranoid schizophrenic with a history of serious violence (he had killed five people). Dr Egdell was a consultant psychiatrist, whom the claimant, *W*, had consulted for the purpose of a possible mental health review tribunal. Dr Egdell concluded that *W* had a long-standing obsession with home-made bombs, and continued to pose a danger to the public. Dr Egdell became concerned that the medical officer responsible for treating *W* had under-estimated the risk he posed. He forwarded a copy of his report to the assistant medical director of the hospital at which *W* was being treated.

Both Scott J and the Court of Appeal held that the disclosure had been justified in the public interest. Bingham LJ held that a psychiatrist who became aware, even confidentially:

> of information which leads him, in the exercise of what the court considers to be a sound professional judgment, to fear that [decisions about the release of a mentally-ill person] may be made on the basis of inadequate information and with a real risk of consequent danger to the public[3]

[1] *Beloff v Pressdram Ltd* [1973] 1 All ER 241, 260 (Ungoed-Thomas J).
[2] [1990] Ch 359 (CA).
[3] *Ibid*, 424.

was entitled to communicate those concerns to the responsible authorities. Sir Stephen Brown P thought the information communicated by the doctor was 'vital information, directly relevant to questions of public safety'.[4]

In other cases, the interest has been recognised where the information relates to a convicted paedophile who might pose a risk to children,[5] and of suspicions that a sex offence had been committed by a social worker (though the disclosure was, in that case, held not to be justified).[6] Further cases can readily be imagined. For instance, a doctor might well—in an appropriate case—be justified in disclosing that a patient was suffering from a serious and communicable disease,[7] even if the patient would not consent to that disclosure, if it were necessary to avoid harm to others.[8] Or a doctor might be justified in disclosing that the patient is unfit to drive, where he threatens to do so.[9] The guidance provided by the General Medical Council seems sound:

> Disclosure of personal information without consent may be justified in the public interest where failure to do so may expose the patient or others to risk of death or serious harm. Where the patient or others are exposed to a risk so serious that it outweighs the patient's privacy interest, you should seek consent to disclosure where practicable. If it is not practicable to seek consent, you should disclose information promptly to an appropriate person or authority. You should generally inform the patient before disclosing the information. If you seek consent and the patient withholds it you should consider the reasons for this, if any are provided by the patient. If you remain of the view that disclosure is necessary to protect a third party from death or serious harm, you should disclose information promptly to an appropriate person or authority.[10]

HOW THE BALANCE IS STRUCK

There is a relative paucity of case law showing how the balance is struck in this area. But the cases do demonstrate some principles, and others seem to be a matter of common sense.

As always, it is necessary to consider both sides of the equation: on the one hand the strength and significance of the interests (particularly the *public*

[4] [1990] Ch 359 (CA), 416.

[5] *R v Chief Constable of North Wales Police, ex parte Thorpe* [1999] QB 396 (CA). *Thorpe* is not a case concerning common law confidentiality as such, but there seems little doubt that its recognition of the relevant public interest would apply to confidential information too.

[6] *R (X) v Chief Constable of the West Midlands Police* [2004] EWHC 61 (Admin), [2004] 1 WLR 1518. The case was, again, complicated by the statutory background.

[7] There are statutory obligations of disclosure in relation to certain communicable diseases: Public Health (Control of Diseases) Act 1984. See also The Health Service (Control of Patient Information) Regulations 2002, SI 2002/1438.

[8] See Toulson & Phipps, paras 11–030, 11–031.

[9] *Duncan v Medical Practitioners Disciplinary Committee* [1986] 1 NZLR 513, 521 (Jeffries J).

[10] General Medical Council Guidance: *Confidentiality, Protecting and Providing Information* (2004), para 27.

interest[11]) in confidentiality. This is a factor of 'crucial importance';[12] if it is not considered, the court is looking at only half the picture. On the other side is the risk to public safety. The gravity of that risk—both in terms of the seriousness of the harm that may be caused, and the degree of the risk—are important. The decided cases relate to serious risks: violent killing[13] and the abuse of children or vulnerable adults.[14] The General Medical Council's guidance refers to the risk of 'death or serious harm'.[15]

It is also necessary to consider how solidly based the concerns in question are. It is not merely a matter of honesty, but of the exercise of objective judgment (ultimately, by the court),[16] albeit that the court will take into account the 'considered judgment of a professional man'.[17] In *R (X) v Chief Constable of the West Midlands Police*[18] the police honestly believed that answers given by the applicant during a police interview suggested he had indecently exposed himself. But the court held that a sufficiently objective approach had not been taken. A rigorous approach demands that there be cogent evidence to establish a 'pressing need' for the information to be disclosed, especially where—as, for instance, in the case of allegations of child sex abuse—the consequences of disclosing unfounded suspicions may be serious.[19]

Then it is necessary to consider whether disclosure is required at all. If the risk can be addressed without disclosure,[20] then the defence may not apply. It seems right, too, that a person should generally be given an opportunity to make necessary disclosures of sensitive personal information voluntarily, in a way which may minimise embarrassment or difficulty. That is what the General Medical Council's advice[21] suggests.

Finally, if disclosure is to be made, it ought to be limited to that disclosure that is necessary in order to protect the public interest, such as disclosure to a

[11] *W v Egdell* [1990] Ch 359, 416 (Stephen Brown P).

[12] *R (X) v Chief Constable of the West Midlands Police* [2004] EWHC 61 (Admin), [2004] 1 WLR 1518, [107]. For instance, the court takes into account the fact that disclosure of allegations of sexual misconduct such as child abuse are likely to have very serious consequences for the individual.

[13] *W v Egdell* [1990] Ch 359 (CA).

[14] *R v Chief Constable of North Wales, ex parte Thorpe* [1999] QB 396 (CA); *R (X) v Chief Constable of the West Midlands Police* [2004] EWHC 61 (Admin), [2004] 1 WLR 1518.

[15] General Medical Council Guidance: *Confidentiality, Protecting and Providing Information* (2004), para 27.

[16] *W v Egdell* [1990] Ch 359, 422 (Bingham LJ): 'The answer . . . must turn not on what the doctor thinks but on what the court rules'.

[17] *Ibid.*

[18] [2004] EWHC 61 (Admin), [2004] 1 WLR 1518.

[19] *Re L (Sexual Abuse: Disclosure)* [1999] 1 WLR 299 (CA); *R (D) v Secretary of State for Health* [2006] EWCA Civ 989, [2006] Lloyd's Rep Med. 457; *R v A Police Authority in the Midlands, ex parte LM* [2000] 1 FLR 612.

[20] For instance if, in *R v Chief Constable of North Wales Police, ex parte Thorpe* [1999] QB 396 (CA), the applicant had been willing to leave the caravan site voluntarily, thereby reducing the risk of abuse to children. In *X v Y* [1988] 2 All ER 648, 656, Rose J pointed out that any risk to the public from the HIV infection of 2 doctors was 'in practice, removed by counselling'. Public disclosure was held unjustified.

[21] Above n 10.

proper authority,[22] or (exceptionally) to a private individual capable of acting upon it.[23] It would be a very exceptional case indeed where general public disclosure was justified under this head (rather than as an aspect of freedom of expression).[24]

[22] As in *W v Egdell* [1990] Ch 359 (CA).

[23] As in *R v Chief Constable of North Wales Police, ex parte Thorpe* [1999] QB 396 (CA), where the applicants' convictions were disclosed to the caravan site owner.

[24] In X *v* Y [1988] 2 All ER 648, Rose J rejected a suggestion that it was in the public interest for information about the HIV infection of 2 doctors to be generally disclosed. But appropriate disclosure to particular affected patients might clearly be justified.

§ 14

Public Interest: Administration of Justice

(1) Information is not protected if its disclosure is necessary to the fair determination of civil rights and obligations or criminal charges, and that interest outweighs the public interest in confidentiality.

(2) Subject to paragraph (3), the question whether the balance of public interests favours disclosure is to be addressed on the particular facts of each case in which it arises.

(3) Exceptionally, information will be protected despite its importance for the fair determination of civil rights and obligations or criminal charges because—

(a) it is within a category of information recognised as being subject to some form of privilege; or

(b) it is within a class of information recognised as being, as a class, subject to public interest immunity.

THE INTEREST RECOGNISED

THERE CAN BE no doubt that there is a public interest in the due administration of justice—civil and criminal[1]—which may take precedence over confidentiality rights. That is, indeed, a matter of Convention right,[2] but it is also a common law policy. It is reflected in a number of different areas of the law. Here, more than anywhere else, the public interest tends to be encapsulated and crystallised in a number of specific rules, rather than simply left to be assessed in each particular case. The underlying effect of those rules, however, is consistent with the general principle stated in § 14.

[1] Including the administration of justice abroad: *Pharaon v Bank of Credit and Commerce International SA* [1998] 4 All ER 455.

[2] European Convention on Human Rights, Art 6.

PROVISION OF EVIDENCE UNDER COMPULSION

Subject to a small number of qualifications (the rules traditionally known as 'privilege'), the law generally attaches great weight to the principle that a criminal or civil court must be in a position to be informed of all evidence necessary to decide a case fairly. Accordingly, a court has power to order parties or third parties to disclose documents or give evidence of confidential matters (unless they are privileged). In that sense confidentiality is 'no answer' to an order for inter-partes or third party disclosure, or to a witness summons, and does not provide a ground for refusing to answer a question. And, of course, once a person is ordered to provide such evidence, the order itself constitutes a complete answer to any private law claim for breach of confidence.[3]

That bald statement, however, may be somewhat misleading, for three reasons. First, although the court has power to require evidence of confidential matters to be given, before exercising that power it will strike a balance (in the particular case) between the confidentiality interests involved and the importance of the evidence being made available. The Judge is expected 'to weigh on the one hand the respect due to confidence in the profession and on the other hand the ultimate interest of the community in justice being done'.[4] In general, the disclosure of confidential information will only be required where 'not only it is relevant but also it is a proper and, indeed, necessary question in the course of justice'.[5] The balance must be struck having regard to all the relevant circumstances of the case, and in particular to the nature and degree of the confidentiality interest at stake. Thus, for example, since orders requiring journalists to disclose their sources interfere with their rights under Article 10,[6] there is special statutory protection,[7] and particularly strong grounds would be required before ordering such disclosure.[8]

Secondly, there are specific categories of privilege that protect certain types of confidential information, and which reflect a view that the interests in preserving confidence consistently take precedence, in a few particular cases, over the interests of justice. The most prominent is legal professional privilege, which

[3] See § 9.

[4] *Attorney-General v Mulholland* [1963] 2 QB 477 (CA), 490 (Lord Denning MR), approved in *British Steel Corp v Granada Television Ltd* [1981] AC 1096 (HL), 1169 (Lord Wilberforce).

[5] *Attorney-General v Mulholland* [1963] 2 QB 477 (CA), 489 (Lord Denning MR). The test whether disclosure is 'necessary' in the interests of justice was also applied to the disclosure of documents in *Dolling Baker v Merrett* [1990] 1 WLR 1205 (CA).

[6] *Goodwin v United Kingdom* (1996) 22 EHRR 123.

[7] Contempt of Court Act 1981, s 10.

[8] The test under s 10 of the Contempt of Court Act 1981 is whether disclosure is 'necessary'—which means something more than 'convenient' and something less than 'indispensable': *Re An Inquiry under the Company Securities (Insider Dealing) Act 1985* [1988] AC 660 (HL), 704 (Lord Griffiths), 708–09 (Lord Oliver). The application of that test is not, however, uniform. Contrast, eg, *Ashworth Hospital Authority v MGN Ltd* [2002] UKHL 29, [2002] 1 WLR 2033, where disclosure was ordered, with *John v Express Newspaper plc* [2000] 1 WLR 1931 (CA), where it was not.

normally applies even where disclosure might avoid the risk of a serious miscarriage of justice.[9] The privilege 'cannot be set aside on the ground that some higher public interest requires that to be done'.[10]

Legal professional privilege represents the gold standard of privileges, in the sense that it is almost unqualified. But other privileges exist which also protect strong public interests in confidentiality being preserved. In particular, privilege attaches to statements (so-called 'without prejudice' communications) made confidentially in the course of settlement discussions, reflecting a public policy that free and candid negotiations should be encouraged.[11] Although subject to more numerous exceptions than legal professional privilege,[12] mere relevance is not an exception, and the rule undoubtedly operates in some cases to prevent highly relevant evidence being placed before the court.

> It is of course distasteful for this or any court to avert its eyes from an admission which, subject to any point about value, appears to incriminate [a party] in lying in a sworn document. However, in the tension between two powerful public interests, it seems to me that that in favour of the protection of the privilege of without prejudice discussions holds sway—unless the privilege is itself abused on the occasion of its exercise.[13]

That comment neatly shows how the privilege operates as, in effect, a consistent (if sometimes surprising) way of balancing the public interest that negotiations should be confidential against the public interest in accurate judicial decision-making.

Thirdly, there is one particular 'privilege'[14] which directly requires a balancing of the public interest in fair proceedings against some other public interest underlying confidentiality. The essence[15] of the immunity is that the court should not require disclosure of documents (or evidence) if the 'harm done to the nation or the public service' by such disclosure would outweigh the 'public interest in the administration of justice'.[16] The courts 'have . . . a power and duty to hold a balance' between these two interests.[17] The overall result, as stated by

[9] See *R v Derby Magistrates Court, ex parte B* [1996] AC 487 (HL). In a criminal case the solution might be to stay proceedings on grounds that no fair trial is possible, but that can hardly be done in civil proceedings.

[10] *Three Rivers DC v Bank of England* (*No 6*) [2004] UKHL 48, [2005] 1 AC 610, [25] (Lord Scott).

[11] *Rush & Tompkins Ltd v GLC* [1989] AC 1280 (HL), 1299 (Lord Griffiths); *Cutts v Head* [1984] Ch 290 (CA), 306 (Oliver LJ).

[12] See *Unilever plc v Procter & Gamble Co* [2000] 1 WLR 2436 (CA), 2444 (Robert Walker LJ).

[13] *Savings and Investment Bank Ltd v Fincken* [2003] EWCA Civ 1630, [2004] 1 WLR 667, [62] (Rix LJ).

[14] Though the term is probably not strictly accurate: see Malek et al (eds), *Phipson on Evidence,* 16th edn (London, 2005), para 25–08.

[15] This book makes no attempt to describe the doctrine in detail. For further information see Malek et al (eds), *Phipson on Evidence,* 16th edn (London, 2005) ch 25, and Toulson & Phipps, ch 19.

[16] *Conway v Rimmer* [1968] AC 910 (HL), 940 (Lord Reid).

[17] *Ibid*, 952 (Lord Reid).

Lord Templeman in *R v Chief Constable of West Midlands Police, ex parte Wiley*, is as follows:

> If a document is relevant and material then it must be disclosed unless it is confidential and unless a breach of confidentiality will cause harm to the public interest which outweighs the harm to the interests of justice caused by non-disclosure.[18]

Public interest immunity is applied where there is a real risk that confidential information seriously prejudicial to an important interest such as national security,[19] the proper working of central government,[20] effective prosecution and at least some aspects of internal police functions,[21] the protection of sources and informants,[22] and the maintenance of confidentiality in documents provided to the government under compulsory power.[23]

The question might well be asked: Given that the court always exercises a discretion whether to require evidence to be given of confidential material (as *Attorney-General v Mulholland*[24] holds) and will therefore presumably *always* balance the public interest attaching to confidentiality in a particular case against the public interest in the administration of justice, is there really any need for a separate head of 'public interest immunity' at all? Why cannot the ordinary discretion suffice? The survival of public interest immunity as a special category is partly a matter of historical accident. Historically, the principles *were* distinct: public interest immunity began as 'crown privilege'—a special status-based privilege for central government. It was only gradually that it came to be accepted that it is a privilege related to subject-matter not the status of the person claiming it, and that the court (not the crown) decides how the balance is to be struck. Then, for many years, public interest immunity permitted 'class claims', which attempted to strike the balance without regard to the particular interests engaged in a particular case. But, since *ex parte Wiley*[25] and the 'Arms to Iraq' affair, class claims have been increasingly disfavoured.[26] If all that is required is to balance, case by case, the 'public interest in confidentiality' with the 'interests of justice', then that is capable of being done without any special jargon of 'public interest immunity'. It is not analytically different from the

[18] [1995] 1 AC 274 (HL), 281. See also the approach set out by Lord Bingham in *R v H* [2004] UKHL 3, [2004] 2 AC 134.

[19] *Balfour v Foreign & Commonwealth Office* [1994] 1 WLR 681 (CA).

[20] *Conway v Rimmer* [1968] AC 910 (HL).

[21] See, eg, *R v Chief Constable of West Midlands Police, ex parte Wiley* [1995] 1 AC 274 (HL) (police complaints), *Goodridge v Chief Constable of Hampshire* [1999] 1 All ER 896.

[22] *R v Lewes Justices, ex parte Secretary of State for the Home Department* [1973] AC 388 (HL); *D v National Society for Prevention of Cruelty to Children* [1978] AC 171 (HL); *Chief Constable for Greater Manchester v McNally* [2002] EWCA Civ 14, [2002] 2 Cr App R 169.

[23] *Re Joseph Hargreaves Ltd* [1900] 1 Ch 347, approved by Lord Reid in *Conway v Rimmer* [1968] AC 910, 946. The subsequent decisions discussed by Toulson & Phipps at paras 19–060 to 19–067 are not on any view inconsistent with the proposition that there is *a* public interest in such documents being kept confidential.

[24] [1963] 2 QB 477 (CA), 490.

[25] [1995] 1 AC 274 (HL).

[26] Malek et al (eds). *Phipson on Evidence*, 16th edn (London, 2005), para 25–12.

exercise a court always carries out before ordering the disclosure of confidential information. The determined application of Occam's razor would enable the law to function quite adequately without any special rules for 'public interest immunity'.

There seems to be only one remaining point of distinction which might justify retaining public interest immunity as a distinct category. Although class claims by central government department are now very rare, other authorities 'still can and regularly do make class claims',[27] and such claims are sometimes accepted as such.[28] So long as class claims to public interest immunity are made and upheld, there will remain a distinction between the case-by-case discretion exercised under *Mulholland*,[29] and public interest immunity. But the distinction is probably more theoretical than real: for the rare cases where a class claim to public interest immunity is upheld ought to be cases where all documents in the relevant class will necessarily be documents where the public interest in confidentiality outweighs the public interest in disclosure.

The overall position, then, is that the law on these points has become unnecessarily complex, largely as a result of historical accident. Different parts of it (the law of legal professional privilege, or without prejudice privilege, the discretion to compel production of documents and evidence, and 'crown privilege' as it has mutated into public interest immunity) have grown up in different ways. But if one strips away this luxuriant growth, three principles remain: (*a*) the court will permit (and indeed require) confidential information to be put in evidence where the interests of justice outweigh the public interest in confidentiality; (*b*) in general, that balancing test will be carried out in each particular case and for each item of information; (*c*) in a few cases (which might be called 'class claims', but which include legal professional privilege, without prejudice privilege, and legitimate class claims to public interest immunity) the court regards the public interest in non-disclosure of that class of information as being so strong as to justify a rigid rule excluding the evidence, although that rule is normally subject to exceptions.

VOLUNTARY PROVISION OF EVIDENCE

Parties naturally cannot contract to refuse to provide evidence under compulsion. In any event, a contract will be void as contrary to public policy if it tends to interfere with the due administration of justice.[30] Nevertheless, it seems

[27] *Ibid*. See also *R v Chief Constable of West Midlands Police, ex parte Wiley* [1995] 1 AC 274, 282 (Lord Slynn), pointing out that class claims might in particular situations be justified.

[28] See Malek et al (eds), *Phipson on Evidence*, 16th edn (London, 2005), para 25–07: 'there have been sightings of class claims being made by other bodies being upheld'.

[29] [1963] 2 QB 477 (CA).

[30] *Fulham Football Club Ltd v Cabra Estates plc* [1992] BCC 863 (CA), 864 (Neill LJ); *Compagnie Noga d'Importation et d'Exportation SA v Australia and New Zealand Banking Group Ltd* [2007] EWHC 293 (Comm).

likely that a person could validly contract not to provide evidence *except* under compulsion (ie, not to cooperate voluntarily).[31] What, then, is the position if there is no such express agreement? Can a confidant provide evidence voluntarily, or must she wait to be compelled? The question has never been squarely addressed, and there are conflicting dicta.

It is suggested, as a matter of principle, that a person subject to a duty of confidence will not breach that duty by giving evidence in civil or criminal proceedings, provided the public interest in the administration of justice in fact outweighs the interest in confidentiality. In other words, the person concerned is not obliged to wait for the court to rule that the material in question should be compelled, but will have a defence to a claim for breach of confidence if it would have been compellable.[32] This seems consistent with the view finally reached by Millett J in *Price Waterhouse v BCCI*.[33]

A contrary view, however, appears to have been taken by Munby J in *A Health Authority v X*,[34] and given at least lukewarm endorsement in the Court of Appeal.[35] Munby J said that it was the duty of a doctor 'like that of any other professional or other person who owes a duty of confidentiality to his patient or client' to assert confidentiality and 'put before the court every argument that can properly be put against disclosure'.[36] Munby J's comments were made by way of answer to a criticism that a doctor had acted improperly by resisting disclosure. As such they are salutary; the court will hardly criticise a professional for asking the court to strike the balance in such cases. But as statements of general[37] positive duty, it is suggested, they go too far.[38] The true position, it is suggested, should be that a person who decides to disclose documents because *he* considers the administration of justice requires disclosure does not ipso facto commit a breach of confidence, but acts at his peril. If a court subsequently agrees, then no wrong will have been committed. If a court disagrees, then the discloser will have acted in breach of confidence. For this reason the safest course is no doubt to insist upon an order being made, following which disclosure can safely be made under compulsion.

[31] *Price Waterhouse v BCCI* [1992] BCLC 583.

[32] This is consistent with the view taken in public interest immunity cases since the Scott Report (*Report of the Enquiry into the Export of Defence Equipment and Dual Use Goods to Iraq and Related Prosecutions*, HMSO, London, 1996): it is wrong for the government to assert immunity without regard to the balance to be struck.

[33] [1992] BCLC 583.

[34] [2001] 2 FCR 634.

[35] [2001] EWCA Civ 2014, [2002] 2 All ER 780, [25] (Thorpe LJ).

[36] Quoted at [2002] 2 All ER 780, [7].

[37] An express contractual term or established custom in a particular profession might impose such a duty.

[38] See *Barclays Bank plc v Taylor* [1989] 1 WLR 1066 (CA), holding that a bank is under no obligation to object to or resist an order requiring the production of documents. But contrast *Marcel v Commissioner of Police of the Metropolis* [1992] Ch 225 (CA), where the court seems to have assumed that disclosure of confidential documents by the police without subpoena would have been a breach of confidence. See in particular [1992] Ch 225, 262 (Sir Christopher Slade).

The point does, however, become critical where compulsion is not an option—notably where the confidant is himself a party to proceedings and wishes to use the confidential information in them. If Munby J is right, the confidant may be placed in an invidious position—forced, in effect, to submit to an injustice because of an inability to provide evidence which justice requires should be provided. Sometimes the problem can be avoided by preventing the risk of injustice, while maintaining the confidence.[39] Sometimes it is avoided by means of a doctrine of implied (but, in reality, imputed) waiver on the part of the confidant.[40] But in other cases, where that cannot or should not be done, it is suggested that the person concerned should be free to volunteer the evidence,[41] though (again) acting at his peril. The same position ought also to apply where, for some reason, the evidence (although important) is not capable of being obtained by compulsion.[42]

[39] For instance, a lawyer may not deploy privileged information in the defence of a claim for wasted costs, but injustice (to the lawyer) is avoided by making assumptions in his favour: *Medcalf v Mardell* [2002] UKHL 27, [2003] 1 AC 120. This may, of course, cause grave injustice to the party seeking the order; but that is presumably regarded as less importance because of the high sanctity attached to maintaining legal professional privilege.

[40] As where a client sues his former lawyer: see p 50 above.

[41] As seems to have been assumed by Hirst LJ in *R v Institute of Chartered Accountants for England and Wales, ex parte Brindle* [1994] BCC 297, 312 (disciplinary proceedings). See also *Duncan v Medical Practitioners Disciplinary Committee* [1986] 1 NZLR 513.

[42] For instance, it is doubtful whether foreign arbitration tribunals can compel the production of evidence in England. But a witness with important evidence to give ought to be able to cooperate voluntarily in order to avoid a miscarriage of justice.

§ 15

Public Interest: National Security

Information is not protected to the extent that the public interest in the security of the nation outweighs the public interest in its confidentiality.

THERE SEEMS NO doubt, in principle, that the courts would recognise a strong public interest in national security which would, in an appropriate case, justify disclosure of confidential information.[1] In practice, however, this interest so closely overlaps § 12 (wrongdoing), and arises so rarely, that its ambit as a distinct principle has not been considered.

One would expect it to follow the same pattern as the wrongdoing and public safety exceptions. A balance would have to be struck (objectively and, ultimately, by the court) weighing the national security interest at stake against the public interest in confidentiality with respect to the particular information in question. Disclosure would have to be justifiable both in principle, and by reference to its extent and the person to whom it was made.

[1] See, eg, *Weld-Blundell v Stephens* [1920] AC 956 (HL), 965–6 (Lord Finlay) ('danger to the State . . . may supersede the duty'); *Beloff v Pressdram Ltd* [1973] 1 All ER 241, 260 (Ungoed-Thomas J) ('matters carried out or contemplated, in breach of the country's security').

§ 16

Restraint of Trade

(1) Information is not protected where that would unreasonably restrain trade.
(2) In the absence of any express term, the obligation to keep information confidential after termination of a contract of employment will only be regarded as extending to information which is highly confidential (a 'trade secret'), that is, to information in respect of which the interests of the employer in its continued confidentiality outweigh any restraint on the employee's trade or employment therefrom.
(3) A contract may provide further protection expressly. But such a term will be valid only if it is reasonably required to protect confidential information, and then only if its duration and scope are reasonable.

THE INTERESTS RECOGNISED

BY PREVENTING ACCESS to or use of confidential information, a person can obtain a competitive advantage: the secret formula that enables me alone to produce a drug, the secret manufacturing technique that enables me to produce a product more cheaply or effectively than my competitors, the 'exclusive' story that will attract readers to my newspaper rather than yours. There is a delicate balance to be struck here. On the one hand, enabling people to keep and reap the benefits of these secrets may encourage innovation, reduce prices, or increase quality. On the other hand, reduction of competition and the creation of market power may reduce consumer welfare.[1] In many areas of the law, these issues are addressed directly by the statutory grant of monopolies on limited terms (patents, copyright, design rights and so forth). The law of confidentiality has to address them through other mechanisms.

Protection of confidential information also has knock-on effects in markets other than the one in which the claimant primarily does business. In particular, if employees are precluded from using *any* information acquired by them while

[1] See, for a recognition of the significance of that fact in the context of confidentiality, *Fisher Karpak Industries Ltd v Nichols* [1982] FSR 351, 354 (Whitford J).

working for an employer, they may in practice have little hope of working for anyone else in the same field. That adversely affects the competitiveness of the labour market, and might be thought unfair to the employees themselves. On the other hand, of course, if they were free to leave one employer at any time and take with them and pass on to a new employer everything they knew about their old employer's business, that would fatally undermine the public benefits that can flow from confidentiality—as set out above—and be unfair to the old employer. Some balance has to be struck between protecting an employer's legitimate business secrets, and utterly undermining employees' ability to acquire skills and knowledge that they may transfer to new employment.

The common law addresses that problem partly by the manipulation of implied terms, and partly through the restraint of trade doctrine, scrutinising even agreed terms that would:

> deprive [the employee] for a lengthened period of the power of employing, in any part of the United Kingdom, that mechanical and technical skill and knowledge which . . . his own industry, observation, and intelligence have enabled him to acquire . . . thus forcing him to begin life afresh, as it were, and depriving him of the means of supporting himself and his family.[2]

This is not a matter merely of unfairness to the employee, since:

> it is in the public interest that a man should be free to exercise his skill and experience to the best advantage for the benefit of himself and of all those who desire to employ him.[3]

As so often, then, there is a balance to be struck. In practical terms, it has largely fallen to be struck in one particular context: that of the former employee who leaves to work for a competitor or to set up in her own right as a competitor of her former employer. It has produced a body of case law that is specialised to deal with this particular context. One should start with that case law.

USE OF INFORMATION BY FORMER EMPLOYEES

The disclosure of confidential information by *current* employees gives rise to no great difficulty. They are already gainfully employed. They owe duties of loyalty to their employer. The competitive economy is not conspicuously harmed by holding them strictly to these duties with regard to any information the employer wishes to have kept confidential. Questions of competition and the free market intrude, however, once the employment ends. At that point, it becomes necessary to define the extent of the employee's continuing duty to

[2] *Herbert Morris Ltd v Saxelby* [1916] 1 AC 688 (HL), 698–9.

[3] *Ibid*, 699 (Lord Atkinson). See also *Fisher Karpak Industries Ltd v Nichols* [1982] FSR 351, 354 (Whitford J): 'it must be quite wrong to impose a restraint which is effectively going to operate to stop a man using his acquired skills rather than to stop him using information which he ought never to have taken into use at all'.

keep secret information confidential, but to do so in a way that limits the employer's ability to sterilise the former employee's ability to compete in the labour market.

As it has developed, the case law draws a distinction between two categories of confidential information. On the one hand, there are 'trade secrets', and 'material . . . of such a highly confidential nature as to require the same protection as a trade secret'.[4] Employees will be subject to an implied term that they will not, after the employment ceases, make use of a 'trade secret'. On the other hand lies information which, although confidential (and often protected from disclosure so long as the employment lasted) is not thought worthy of protection once the employment relationship has ended. Employees will not be prevented from making use of such confidential information that is not a 'trade secret'.

The attempt to draw a categorical distinction between 'trade secrets' and other information, and the use of terminology in this area, is open to criticism.[5] It is tolerable, however, provided one understands the true nature of the inquiry. In *Faccenda Chicken*[6] the Court of Appeal in fact made it clear that the nature of the information is only one part of the picture. Although, as a matter of short-hand, it has become customary to refer to protected information as 'trade secrets', the true position is that the court considers a number of factors all tending to the same overall question: Would preventing the use or disclosure of particular information impose anunreasonable restriction on the ex-employee's ability to find or carry out work in the sector in which he is skilled?[7] Thus what appears to be a question of categorisation along a bright line ('trade secret or not?') is in reality a question of fact and degree.[8]

In broad terms one would expect this inquiry to be carried out by comparing, on the one hand, the strength of the employer's interest in continued confidentiality, and on the other hand, the extent to which continued confidentiality could be expected to hamper the employee. And it turns out that, among the various factors that are explicitly[9] or implicitly identified, all seem to bear on one or other side of this balance.

Thus, looking at the employer's interests, the key variables are how strong the expectations of confidentiality were, and how much damage would be done to the employer's business if the information were used or disclosed. The essence of a 'trade secret' is that it is information that is kept confidential and used in the employer's business, and whose disclosure 'would be liable to cause real (or significant) harm to the owner of the secret'.[10] The court, in this context, is really considering the strength that ought to be accorded to the employer's expectation

[4] *Faccenda Chicken Ltd v Fowler* [1987] Ch 117 (CA), 137 (Neill LJ).

[5] See, eg, Dean, 196–8.

[6] [1987] Ch 117.

[7] Toulson & Phipps, para 14–014.

[8] *PSM International plc v Whitehouse* [1992] IRLR 279 (CA), 282 (Lloyd LJ).

[9] For instance, by Neill LJ in *Faccenda Chicken Ltd v Fowler* [1987] Ch 117 (CA), 137–8, where 4 factors are identified.

[10] *Lansing Linde Ltd v Kerr* [1991] 1 WLR 251 (CA), 260 (Staughton LJ).

of confidentiality. The court takes into account matters such as the nature of the employment,[11] the degree to which the employer has taken steps to impress the employees that the information is confidential,[12] the extent to which the information is kept secret from the public[13] or is truly difficult to discover,[14] and how seriously the employer would suffer if the information were used or disclosed.[15] Protectable information includes trade secrets in the strict sense, including such things as the ingredients of chemical compounds and other sophisticated products,[16] but also information such as details of customer accounts,[17] future business strategy,[18] and confidential financial information about the employer.

That deals with the employer's side. On the other side, one has to consider the extent to which protection will damage the employee's interests. Here, a key question is the extent to which the employee will be capable of working without using the information in question. Thus a distinction is drawn between things such as 'a man's aptitudes, his skill, his dexterity, his manual or mental ability'[19] and concrete information specific to the former *employer's* business, which a person could perform perfectly well without.[20] The courts also consider how far the information in question forms a definable separate body of knowledge,[21] capable of being put on one side, as it were, in subsequent employment. Unless the employer can establish a 'separate body of objective knowledge',[22] the damage done to the employee's ability to exercise her skills and aptitudes is likely to be too great to justify protection. It also follows that the use of information in a particular form (such as a plan, or a list of customers[23]) is more likely to be pro-

[11] That is, whether it is an employment of the sort where confidentiality is regarded as a usual and important aspect of the job: *Faccenda Chicken Ltd v Fowler* [1987] Ch 117 (CA), 137 (Neill LJ).

[12] *Ibid*, 138 (Neill LJ), citing E *Worsley & Co Ltd v Cooper* [1939] 1 All ER 290, 307 (Morton J), but cf *Lancashire Fires Ltd v SA Lyons & Co Ltd* [1996] FSR 629 (CA).

[13] *FSS Travel & Leisure Services Ltd v Johnson* [1999] FSR 505 (CA), 512 (Mummery LJ).

[14] See, eg, *A T Poeton (Gloucester Plating) Ltd v Horton* [2001] FSR 14 (CA), [34]. Morritt LJ was (barely) willing to assume that a design was a 'trade secret', but did not regard it as worthy of post-termination protection since its features were almost entirely based on publicly available information, or obvious inferences from such information.

[15] *FSS Travel & Leisures Services Ltd v Johnson* [1999] FSR 505 (CA), 512 (Mummery LJ).

[16] *SBJ Stephenson Ltd v Mandy* [2000] FSR 286, 298 (Bell J). Classic examples include chemical formulae (*Amber Size and Chemical Co Ltd v Menzel* [1913] 2 Ch 239) or manufacturing processes (*Reid & Sigrist Ltd v Moss and Mechanism Ltd* (1932) 49 RPC 461; *Lancashire Fires Ltd v SA Lyons & Co Ltd* [1996] FSR 629 (CA)).

[17] *SBJ Stephenson Ltd v Mandy* [2000] FSR 286, 300–01 (Bell J); *Thomas Marshall (Exports) Ltd v Guinle* [1979] Ch 227.

[18] *Littlewoods Organisation Ltd v Harris* [1977] 1 WLR 1472 (CA).

[19] *Herbert Morris Ltd v Saxelby* [1916] 1 AC 688 (HL), 714 (Lord Shaw). Lord Shaw described this as 'subjective knowledge'.

[20] *Herbert Morris Ltd v Saxelby* [1916] 1 AC 688 (HL), 714 (Lord Shaw): 'Trade secrets, the names of customers, all such things which in sound philosophical language are denominated objective knowledge'. See also *Printers & Finishers Ltd v Holloway* [1965] 1 WLR 1, 5.

[21] *Faccenda Chicken Ltd v Fowler* [1987] Ch 317, 338; *FSS Travel & Leisure Systems Ltd* v *Johnson* [1999] FSR 505, 513.

[22] *FSS Travel & Leisure Systems Ltd v Johnson* [1999] FSR 505 (CA), 513 (Mummery LJ).

[23] *Robb v Green* [1895] 2 QB 315 (CA).

tected than similar information that is not in that particular form (such as the general principles upon which a product is manufactured, or the identity of the customers[24]). The use to which the employee intends to put the information ought also to matter: it is one thing to prevent an employee using information to work, another to prevent him from disclosing it for some other purpose.[25]

EXPRESS DUTIES

So much for implied duties. But what if the duty is express?[26] For many years it was assumed that an express term (which could take the form either of a direct term protecting information as confidential, or of an express term preventing competitive activity in order to protect confidential information) might extend protection.[27] In *Faccenda Chicken*, in remarks that were plainly *obiter*, Neill LJ cast doubt on that proposition.[28] But it seems to be correct in principle. Post termination restrictions fall into a grey area, where the extent of protection is unclear. If there is no express term, it seems right that the employee should have the benefit of any doubt; implied protection should extend only to information that is clearly confidential.[29] But if there is an express term, weight should be given to it, and it should be enforced unless it places unreasonable restrictions on the use to which an employee can work or put information. The essential question in each case is the same: How should the balance be struck between the employer's interest (which is also a public interest) in maintaining confidentiality and the employee's interest (which is also a public interest) in being free to make use of her skills and knowledge? But the presence of an express term ought to affect how that balance is struck in various ways.

That seems to be the view taken in cases decided after *Faccenda*.[30] In *AT Poeton (Gloucester Plating) Ltd v Horton*[31] and in *Thomas v Farr plc*[32] the Court of Appeal simply assumed (without discussion) that it was correct: an express covenant to restrain competition or to protect specific information may be valid even if the implied term would not extend to it. That is surely correct,

24 *Roger Bullivant Ltd v Ellis* [1987] ICR 464 (CA), 473–4 (Nourse LJ).

25 The distinction was drawn by Harman J in *Systems Reliability Holdings plc v Smith* [1990] IRLR 377, 384. It appears to have been overlooked in *Mainmet Holdings plc v Austin* [1991] FSR 538, criticised on that ground by Toulson & Phipps, para 14–024.

26 This is an instance of the symmetry question, discussed above, p 56.

27 See, in particular, *Printers & Finishers Ltd v Holloway* [1965] 1 WLR 1, 6 (Cross J); *United Sterling Corp Ltd v Felton* [1974] RPC 162, 167 (Brightman J); *Littlewoods Organisation Ltd v Harris* [1977] 1 WLR 1472 (CA), 1479 (Lord Denning MR).

28 [1987] Ch 117 (CA), 137.

29 *Ixora Trading Inc v Jones* [1990] 1 FSR 251, 261 (Mummery J).

30 *Systems Reliability Holdings plc v Smith* [1990] IRLR 377, 384 (Harman J); *Balston Ltd v Headline Filters Ltd* [1987] FSR 330, 347–8 (Scott J). In *Lancashire Fires Ltd v S A Lyons & Co Ltd* [1996] FSR 629, 667, Bingham MR left the question open, but the tenor of his comments appears to support the ability of express terms to extend the protection.

31 [2001] FSR 14, [39] (Morritt LJ).

32 [2007] EWCA Civ 118.

for such terms can (*a*) avoid the difficulties in defining what is confidential by expressly defining the relevant information or, in the case of a simple covenant not to compete, obviating the need for such definition and (*b*) strike a much more sophisticated balance in terms of the area and temporal extent than the implied term. The public interest still falls to be applied, but it is applied through the conventional restraint of trade tests applied to the express term.

APPLICATION IN OTHER CONTEXTS

The thesis advanced above is that, despite their specialised form, the common law rules concerning post-termination restraints on employees constitute the application, to a particular context, of the general principle set out in § 11. If that is so, one would expect the basic principles to be applicable in other contexts too.

There certainly are cases where the *Faccenda Chicken* approach has been applied to non-employment relationships. For instance, in *Také Ltd v BSM Marketing Ltd*[33] it was applied to an agency relationship, so that a former agent was precluded from using confidential information about pricing but permitted to use information about customers' preferences, albeit acquired during the agency, in order to compete after it had terminated. Although there is little specific authority on the point,[34] it seems likely that analogous principles would be applied to other professional relationships. For instance, a lawyer will be precluded from using confidential information acquired about one client in advising another; but it is presumably permissible to use general information about an industry acquired while representing one client in other cases.

In theory, the principle might also be applied between competitors (though the balance would obviously be struck differently). For instance, if two competitors agreed that one would use only information about product X, while the other would use only information about product Y, with the object and effect of reserving a monopoly to each in relation to the particular product, such an agreement might well be anticompetitive and (if so) would not be enforced.[35] It is also conceivable that even a unilateral decision to keep information secret could be attacked on this ground. For example, a company manufacturing a computer might, by keeping details of its operation secret, attempt to obtain market power in relation to products designed to operate with the computer, or

[33] [2006] EWHC 1085 (QB).

[34] In *Regina Glass Fibre Ltd v Schuller* [1972] RPC 229 (CA), 235, Lord Denning MR doubted that a licence to use confidential information would normally be construed to prevent the licensee continuing his business after termination, and appears to have applied some sort of presumption that it would not be in construing the contract there in issue.

[35] Though this would very likely follow not from the common law alone, but from the Competition Act 1998, s 2, or Art 81 EC.

in relation to software.[36] It is at least conceivable that a defendant who somehow obtained such information might be able to argue that the public interest precluded enforcement of the confidentiality obligations, though it is likely that in doing so the defendant would rely primarily on specific provisions of competition law.[37] Such possibilities, however, have not been explored in the case law.

[36] In Case T-201/04 *Microsoft Corp* (17 Sep 2007) the Court of First Instance upheld a decision by the Commission that required technical information to be made available by a dominant firm to its competitors.

[37] In particular Art 82 EC and s 18 of the Competition Act 1998 (abuse of dominant position).

§ 17

Freedom of Expression

Information is not protected where the defendant is exercising a right to freedom of expression, unless restriction of that right is necessary in a democratic society in the interests of national security, the protection of the reputation or rights of others, or for preventing the disclosure of information received in confidence.

QUESTIONS OF TAXONOMY

FOR MANY YEARS, 'freedom of expression' was treated as an aspect of the public interest defence generally (§ 11). Indeed, it was very often addressed indirectly, in the course of asking—for instance—whether a public interest in exposing wrongdoing justified publication to the general public rather than disclosure to a particular regulator. That led sometimes to very broad statements of a public interest in 'knowing the truth',[1] or to rather unstructured invocations of a public interest in knowing some particular aspect of the truth,[2] for instance that wrongdoing be 'exposed'.[3]

This approach, it is suggested, ought now to be avoided. Freedom of expression is not just an aspect of the public interest: it is a human right under Article 10 of the Convention. Notwithstanding Lord Goff's complacency in *Spycatcher* that the traditional approach of English law and that under the Convention would not lead to different conclusions,[4] they certainly have very different starting points. The traditional approach generally sought some positive public interest in publication: the exposure of wrongdoing, or of some item of information that it was vital for the public to know. That tended to divert the inquiry

[1] *Woodward v Hutchins* [1977] 1 WLR 760 (CA), 764 (Lord Denning MR).

[2] As, eg, in *Lion Laboratories Ltd v Evans* [1985] QB 526 (CA).

[3] *Ibid*, 550 (Griffiths LJ).

[4] [1990] 1 AC 109, 284. The complacency is questionable in any event, since the common law undoubtedly arrived at conclusions which were *not* consistent with the Convention. See, eg, *Goodwin v United Kingdom* (1996) 22 EHRR 123; *Observer and Guardian v United Kingdom* (1991) 14 EHRR 153. The majority decision in *Schering Chemicals Ltd v Falkman Ltd* [1982] QB 1 (CA) is another example of a case that was very probably wrong.

from one which sought to ascertain whether confidentiality was a sufficient reason to prevent publication to one in which the court asked whether publication would serve some pressing public interest.[5] Although the presence of such an ulterior advantage may be important to how the balance is struck under Article 10, it is not in any sense necessary. The mere fact that the defendant wishes to provide information to the public is sufficient, in itself, to engage Article 10. Freedom of expression is not merely a right secreted in the interstices of a body of rules designed to protect other aspects of the public interest.

However, it is also desirable to avoid lurching to the opposite extreme. It would be possible to regard every occasion of disclosure as an instance of 'expression', and address all of them under the rubric of Article 10. But it seems strained to analyse the conduct of a person who wishes to report suspicions in confidence to, say, the police or a specific authority under the rubric of 'freedom of expression'.[6] The focus of Article 10 is on public discourse—the freedom to 'receive and impart ideas'[7] which forms 'one of the essential foundations of a democratic society'.[8] Even if it were possible to shoehorn into Article 10 those cases where limited disclosure is justified in the public interest into Article 10,[9] it seems unhelpful to do so. The better approach seems to be to treat Article 10 as applicable primarily to those cases where the defendant's activity involves disclosure in a form that could fairly be regarded as public speech, recognising that there are occasions on which *public* speech would be unjustifiable, but where some other aspect of the public interest (not freedom of expression, as such) warrants limited disclosure.

So understood, the right to freedom of expression constitutes a defence to an action for breach of confidence that is, in principle, distinct from the public interest defence (§ 11), albeit closely related, historically and as a matter of practice. The former tends to apply to specific and narrow disclosures, the latter to general and public disclosures. There may be cases where they overlap; but in principle they are distinct.

HOW ARTICLE 10 APPLIES

By the time, in a confidentiality case, that one comes to consider Article 10, it is always clear that there is at least one possible justification for a restriction on rights of freedom of expression, since Article 10 (2) permits restrictions which

[5] See, eg, *Schering Chemicals Ltd v Falkman* [1982] 1 QB 1 (CA), in which Lord Denning's approach would now be correct.

[6] It would, indeed, be impossible to do so in those cases which concerned the disclosure *by a public authority* of information, since the state is not itself the beneficiary of convention rights.

[7] European Convention on Human Rights, Art 10.

[8] *Handyside v United Kingdom* (1976) 1 EHRR 737, para 49.

[9] As a purely technical matter, at least some expressions of opinion which would not be described as 'publication' do engage Art 10. See, eg, *K v Austria,* Commission Rep of 13 Oct 1992, A255–B, in which Art 10 was applied to giving evidence in court. But see n 6 on the position of public authorities.

are 'necessary in a democratic society, in the interests of national security . . . for the protection of the reputation or rights of others' or 'for preventing the disclosure of information received in confidence'. Once a court comes to consider and apply Article 10, it will obviously first have decided that the claimant has either a privacy interest (possibly engaging Article 8 of the Convention) or an interest through a confidential relationship which might, in theory, justify restriction on one of these grounds, and in the case of a government secret possibly also an interest in national security.

In order to pass muster under Article 10 (2), a restriction on speech must meet three criteria. First, it must be prescribed by law. That requirement poses no difficulty in confidentiality cases: the law of confidentiality constitutes the prescribed legal basis. Secondly, it must serve one of the identified grounds of restriction. That again, as set out above, poses no difficulty, since at least one of the permissible grounds for restriction will apply once the court has identified that the claimant has a reasonable expectation of confidentiality worthy, in principle, of protection. Thirdly, it must be 'necessary in a democratic society'. It is with that question that a court considering Article 10 will primarily be concerned.

The proper approach to that question was explained by Lord Bingham in *R v Shayler,* summarizing the case law of the European Court of Human Rights:

> 'Necessary' has been strongly interpreted: it is not synonymous with 'indispensable', neither has it the flexibility of such expressions as 'admissible', 'ordinary', 'useful', 'reasonable' or 'desirable': *Handyside v United Kingdom*[10] . . . One must consider whether the interference complained of corresponded to a pressing social need, whether it was proportionate to the legitimate aim pursued and whether the reasons given by the national authority to justify it are relevant and sufficient under Article 10 (2): *Sunday Times v United Kingdom.*[11] [12]

Conducting that exercise requires careful consideration to be paid to two questions. On one side of the balance, it is necessary to consider the importance that should be attached in the particular case to freedom of expression. It is clear from the case law of the European Court of Human Rights that not all 'expression' warrants the same level of protection. There is a spectrum: at one end one finds serious speech on matters of political importance, whose protection goes to the very heart of 'democratic society'. It is of 'the very highest importance in any country which lays claim to being a democracy', so that restrictions upon it 'need to be examined rigorously by all concerned'.[13] The spectrum then continues through artistic speech, which is protected but (in practice) less rigorously,[14]

[10] (1976) 1 EHRR 737, [48].

[11] (1979) 2 EHRR 245, [62].

[12] [2002] UKHL 11, [2003] 1 AC 247, [23].

[13] *R (Prolife Alliance) v British Broadcasting Corporation* [2003] UKHL 23, [2004] 1 AC 185, [6] (Lord Nicholls).

[14] For the protection of artistic speech see *Müller v Switzerland* (1988) 13 EHRR 212; for comments on the lower degree of protection, see Lester and D Pannick (eds), *Human Rights Law and Practice,* 2nd edn (London, 2004), para 4.10.15.

commercial speech[15] and celebrity gossip, and down to matters such as pornography, which 'comes well below celebrity gossip in the hierarchy of speech which deserves the protection of the law.'[16] Even restrictions on pornography must be 'necessary in a democratic society'. But it is easier to justify restrictions as proportionate where the speech concerned is at the bottom end of the spectrum of concern than when it is at the top.

On the other side of the scale, it is necessary to analyse carefully the weight and importance to be attached to the ground of restriction in the particular case—the degree to which restricting publication serves a 'pressing social need'. Thus, for example, information whose disclosure might harm national security in some way falls on a spectrum:

> If the issue concerns the disclosure of documents bearing a high security classification and there is apparently credible unchallenged evidence that disclosure is liable to lead to the identification of agents or the compromise of informers, the court may very well be unwilling to intervene. If, at the other end of the spectrum, it appears that while disclosure of the material may cause embarrassment or arouse criticism, it will not damage any security or intelligence interest, the court's reaction is likely to be very different.[17]

At one extreme of the spectrum is information which there is a 'pressing social need' to keep secret; at the other end of the spectrum there is no such pressing social need.[18] Similar spectra could be constructed for other types of confidential information.

BURDENS OF PERSUASION

It seems clear in principle that the burden of persuasion generally lies on the person who seeks to justify an interference with freedom of speech: 'freedom of speech is the rule and the regulation of speech is the exception requiring justification'.[19] Such comments are a temptation to treat Article 10 rights as some sort of trump card, or to adopt the motto, 'if in doubt, publish'.

In at least one respect, however, that clearly cannot be right. In many cases of confidentiality, the *defendant's* right of freedom of expression, protected by Article 10, is pitted against the *claimant's* right to respect for private life, protected by Article 8. One or other of those rights must be interfered with, and in either case the interference must be justified. In those circumstances, it was held in *Re S* that four propositions apply:

[15] That is, advertising and the like, where there is a wider latitude in justification: see *Markt Intern Verlag v Germany* (1989) 12 EHRR 161.

[16] *Belfast City Council v Miss Behavin' Ltd* [2007] UKHL 19, [2007] 1 WLR 1420 [38] (Baroness Hale).

[17] *R v Shayler* [2002] UKHL 11, [2003] 1 AC 247, [33] (Lord Bingham).

[18] See also *Campbell v MGN Ltd* [2004] UKHL 22, [2004] 2 AC 457, [118] (Lord Hope), referring to 'the fact that there are different degrees of privacy'.

[19] *Reynolds v Times Newspapers Ltd* [2001] 2 AC 127 (HL), 208 (Lord Steyn).

> First, neither article has *as such* precedence over the other. Secondly, where the values under the two articles are in conflict, an intense focus on the comparative importance of the specific rights being claimed in the individual case is necessary. Thirdly, the justifications for interfering with or restricting each right must be taken into account. Finally, the proportionality test must be applied to each.[20]

That approach has since been applied in a number of cases.[21]

The same position would presumably apply where Article 10 conflicted with some other qualified Convention right. But does it apply generally? Or is it restricted to cases where one Convention right is pitted against another?

To some extent, of course, the approach must be different. Where permitting publication would not interfere with any Convention right it is meaningless to consider the justification for interfering with 'each right' or to apply a proportionality test 'to each'. But the basic proposition that Article 10 is not a trump card holds good. Even where the ground of restriction is not a *Convention* right, but some other right or interest, an 'intense focus' is still required. The question does not ultimately turn on any burden of proof, or even of persuasion, but on the proper application of the proportionality test in the circumstances of the particular case. The mere invocation of Article 10 is never enough to decide a case. The Human Rights Act directs the court to have 'particular regard' to freedom of expression.[22] But this does not require the court to give any special or extra weight to freedom of expression in such contexts, only that it be specifically considered.[23]

THE FACTORS

Because the application of Article 10 depends on a balancing exercise which is carried out on a case-by-case basis, and in an infinite variety of circumstances, it would be wrong to attempt to identify every relevant factor, or to reduce the exercise to rigid rules. Nevertheless, common sense and authority help to identify a number of recurring, and sometimes overlapping, themes. In broad terms the factors are relevant to one of the two questions identified above: What is the strength of the defendant's rights under Article 10? And what is the strength of the claimant's rights or interests?

The type and subject-matter of the speech. As explained above, English and European case law recognises that all speech is not equally valuable, and that

[20] [2004] UKHL 47, [2005] 1 AC 593, [17] (Lord Steyn), summarising the conclusions of the House of Lords in *Campbell v MGN Ltd* [2004] UKHL 22, [2004] 2 AC 457. See also *Douglas v Hello Ltd* [2001] QB 967, [135] (Sedley LJ).

[21] *Lord Browne of Madingley v Associated Newspapers Ltd* [2007] EWCA Civ 295, [2007] 3 WLR 289, [39]; *McKennitt v Ash* [2006] EWCA Civ 1714, [2007] 3 WLR 194, [46]–[48]; *HRH Prince of Wales v Associated Newspapers Ltd* [2006] EWCA Civ 1776, [2007] 3 WLR 222, [52]; *X & Y v Persons Unknown* [2006] EWHC 2783 (QB), [2007] HRLR 4, [27] (Eady J).

[22] Human Rights Act 1998, s 12 (4).

[23] *Ashdown v Telegraph Group Ltd* [2001] Ch 685, [34] (Morritt V-C).

some types of speech are therefore more rigorously protected than others. Freedom of expression is at its most powerful where it seeks to communicate serious and important information and ideas to the public, to make a 'contribution . . . to a debate of general interest'.[24] Obviously that applies strongly to speech which is directed at politics or public affairs in the strictest sense, such as the actual workings of government,[25] but the principle goes wider. Thus a strong public interest has been recognised in the expression of information regarding the administration of justice,[26] the potentially dangerous activities of religious groups,[27] or conditions and behaviour in schools,[28] and secure mental hospitals.[29] Further down the spectrum are cases concerning commercial wrongdoing (or alleged wrongdoing), such as alleged corruption in a sport,[30] or corporate fraud or mismanagement.[31] Still further down the spectrum is speech about 'celebrities' and their personal lives.[32] Right at the bottom of the spectrum would lie expressions about the personal activities of ordinary people in which there is no real public interest. For instance, although in *Campbell v MGN Ltd*[33] the House of Lords accepted that it was legitimate to publish information about a model's drug treatment, bearing in mind her own previous comments on the issue and her status as a role model for young people, it was made quite clear that information concerning the drug treatment of a private individual with no public profile would not have been protected.

The degree to which the proposed publication will add to information already available to the public. This factor is somewhat double-edged. On the one hand, where a large amount of information has already been made available to the public on a particular topic, the addition of some further details might add sufficiently little to it that it does not constitute a major intrusion on confidentiality.[34] That tells in favour of permitting publication. On the other hand, if the relevant information is already in the public domain, so that little more will be added by additional publication, that reduces the significance of the proposed publication, since it will not impart much more information than is already

[24] *von Hannover v Germany* (2005) 40 EHRR 1, [76].

[25] As in *Attorney-General v Jonathan Cape Ltd* [1976] QB 752, or *Attorney-General v Guardian Newspapers Ltd (No 2)* [1990] 1 AC 109 (HL). Also commercial matters affecting government: *London Regional Transport v The Mayor of London* [2001] EWCA Civ 1491, [2003] EMLR 4.

[26] *Lion Laboratories Ltd v Evans* [1985] QB 526 (CA) (accuracy of breathalyzer equipment).

[27] *Hubbard v Vosper* [1972] QB 84 (CA).

[28] *Leeds City Council v Channel Four Television* [2005] EWHC 3522 (Fam), [42] (Munby J).

[29] *Mersey Care NHS Trust v Ackroyd* [2007] EWCA Civ 101, [32] (Clarke MR).

[30] *Jockey Club v Buffham* [2002] EWHC 1866 (QB), [2003] QB 462, [47] (Gray J).

[31] *Cream Holdings Ltd v Bannerjee* [2004] UKHL 44, [2005] 1 AC 253; *Lord Browne of Madingley v Associated Newspapers Ltd* [2007] EWCA Civ 295, [2007] 3 WLR 289.

[32] *A v B plc* [2002] EWCA Civ 337, [2003] QB 195, [43] (activities of professional footballers off the pitch had a 'modicum' of public interest); *Campbell v MGN Ltd* [2004] UKHL 22, [2004] 2 AC 457.

[33] *Ibid.*

[34] See, eg, *Barrymore v News Group Newspapers Ltd* [1997] FSR 600, 603: given widespread public knowledge that *B* was gay, publishing the bare fact that he had been involved in a gay relationship was not a major intrusion.

available.[35] This seems to have been the view taken by the majority in *Campbell v MGN Ltd*[36]—the balance between what a photograph would add to the information being published textually, and the intrusion it would cause, told against permitting publication.

Similar arguments sometimes arise where the information in question is intended imminently to be made public. That is obviously not a bar to protection. A famous hypothetical example concerns military secrets. The plans for the D-Day landings were undoubtedly highly protectable on 4 June 1944. But more common cases involve commercial information—such as the plot of a forthcoming play,[37] the cover of a forthcoming record album,[38] or the contents of a forthcoming novel.[39] In such cases the public gains little useful information if the information is published slightly earlier—a factor which ought to tell in favour of restraining a pre-emptive strike which will damage the claimant's commercial interests without significantly adding to the store of public knowledge.[40]

Whether the proposed publication is of accurate information. For reasons explained above (§ 3) information may be protected as confidential even if it is false. But its accuracy is obviously important when it comes to considering freedom of expression, since there is plainly a greater need to protect the right to receive accurate information than there is to protect the circulation of inaccurate rumour. It does not follow that it would never be a defence for, say, a journalist to rely on Article 10 when the information that had been published turned out to be inaccurate. That would be inconsistent with the rule, under the Convention, that it may be a disproportionate interference with freedom of expression to require a person to prove the truth of what she said.[41] But, by analogy to the position in defamation cases,[42] it is likely that in a case where the information published was false, the publisher would be expected to establish not only a bona fide belief in its accuracy, but that the publication was a matter of 'responsible journalism'. As Lord Nicholls put it in *Bonnick v Morris:*

> [r]esponsible journalism is the point at which a fair balance is held between freedom of expression on matters of public concern and the reputations of individuals.[43]

[35] This approach was taken in X (*a woman formerly known as Mary Bell*) *v News Group Newspapers Ltd* [2003] EWHC 1101 (QB), [2003] EMLR 37, [53].

[36] [2004] UKHL 22, [2004] 2 AC 457.

[37] *Gilbert v Star Newspaper Ltd* (1894) 11 TLR 4.

[38] *Creation Records Ltd v News Group Newspapers Ltd* [1997] EMLR 444.

[39] *Bloomsbury Publishing Ltd v News Group Newspapers Ltd* [2003] EWHC 1205 (Ch), [2003] 1 WLR 1633; *Times Newspapers Ltd v MGN Ltd* [1993] EMLR 443 (CA).

[40] This seems to have been the approach of Bingham MR in *Times Newspapers Ltd v MGN Ltd* [1993] EMLR 443, 447. The case concerned advance publication of information from Margaret Thatcher's memoirs; an injunction was refused on other grounds.

[41] See, eg, *Lingens v Austria* (1986) 8 EHRR 407, [46].

[42] *Reynolds v Times Newspapers Ltd* [2001] 2 AC 127 (HL); *Bonnick v Morris* [2002] UKPC 31, [2003] 1 AC 300; *Jameel v Wall Street Journal Europe sprl* [2006] UKHL 44, [2006] 3 WLR 642.

[43] *Ibid*, [23]. See also the position taken by the European Court of Human Rights in, eg, *Bladet Tromsø v Norway* (1999) 29 EHRR 125.

It is unlikely that Article 10 would be held to protect the publication of confidential information that was both inaccurate and not responsibly reported.

The extent to which the claimant is a public figure or has chosen to enter the public arena on a particular topic. A public figure is entitled to have a private life.[44] Individuals do not, by encouraging or permitting media interest, make every aspect of their lives matters 'of public interest'.[45] Thus, in *Campbell v MGN Ltd*,[46] Lord Hoffman rejected the proposition that 'the fact that [Naomi Campbell] is a public figure who has had a long and symbiotic relationship with the media' would itself justify publication of details of her drug treatment.[47] But the fact is not irrelevant. Things that would normally be of no public interest may become of public interest where the person to whom they relate occupies an important public position. So, for instance, politicians and civil servants may have to accept a higher degree of scrutiny.[48] So too, if a person chooses to make statements or take public positions on particular issues, it is easier to identify a public interest in the exposure of his actual behaviour in relation to those issues.[49] A claimant can hardly be permitted to use confidentiality in order to prevent the exposure of false statements that he himself has made or caused to be put in the public domain.[50] The balance becomes more delicate as the exposure of false statements shades into the exposure of a 'false image', or of private behaviour inconsistent with a person's public expressions of belief or character. But although press enthusiasm for exposing hypocrisy is sometimes a sanctimonious cover for muck-raking, a person who has chosen to expose some aspect of his life cannot claim to have as strong an expectation of confidentiality in it,[51] and must recognise that it is more likely to be regarded as a matter of 'public interest' than might otherwise be the case.[52] There comes a point—variable and elusive perhaps—at which the exposure of hypocrisy can be said to be in the public interest.[53]

[44] *A v B plc* [2002] EWCA Civ 337, [2003] QB 195, [11 (xii)].

[45] To the extent that some older authorities, such as *Woodward v Hutchins* [1977] 1 WLR 760 (CA) and *Lennon v News Group* [1978] FSR 575 might be read as supporting such a view, they should not be regarded as correct. The point was left open in *Campbell v Frisbee* [2002] EWCA Civ 1375, [2003] ICR 141.

[46] [2004] UKHL 22, [2004] 2 AC 457, [57].

[47] See also *Archer v Williams* [2003] EWHC 1670 (QB), [2003] EMLR 869, [63]–[66] (Jackson J).

[48] *Lingens v Austria* (1986) 8 EHRR 407, [42]. *A v B plc* [2002] EWCA Civ 337, [2003] QB 195, [11 (xii)]: 'The public figure may hold a position where higher standards of conduct can be rightly expected by the public. The public figure may be a role model whose conduct could well be emulated by others.'

[49] Contrast *Archer v Williams* [2003] EWHC 1670 (QB), [2003] EMLR 38, [65]–[66] with *Campbell v MGN Ltd* [2004] UKHL 22, [2004] 2 AC 457. Had there been evidence that Lady Archer had expressed herself publicly *in relation to the matters at issue*, as Ms Campbell had in relation to drugs, the result might have been different.

[50] *Hyde Park Residence Ltd v Yelland* [2001] Ch 143 (CA), [73] (Mance LJ).

[51] *Mills v News Group Newspapers Ltd* [2001] EMLR 41.

[52] As in *Campbell v MGN Ltd* [2004] UKHL 22, [2004] 2 AC 457, where Ms Campbell had made (untrue) public statements concerning her attitude to drugs.

[53] In *McKennit v Ash* [2006] EWCA Civ 1714, [2007] 3 WLR 194, [69], Buxton LJ appears to have thought that it was probably not correct always to insist on a 'high degree' or wrongdoing being

Where it is alleged that a claimant has 'courted publicity' in relation to a particular issue:

> close attention may need to be paid to how . . . information came into the public domain and as to its limits.[54]

Is the claimant truly a 'publicity seeker' or simply 'in the public eye'?[55] Has the claimant been willing to lay bare some aspect of his life, or has he insisted (for instance, in interviews) on keeping some boundaries?[56]

The relationship of the defendant or confidant to the subject-matter of the speech. There is an intuitive difference between a complete stranger seeking to expose the details of, for example, a relationship, and one of the persons in that relationship doing so. Where, directly or indirectly (ie, through the press) somebody seeks to make public information about herself—some aspect of her own life—there are grounds for regarding the rights under Article 10 as more strongly engaged than where a stranger seeks to make the same revelations.[57] Indeed, it seems arguable that Article 8 is also engaged in such cases—since the right to 'privacy' is not merely a right to be left alone, but a positive right to develop one's sense of identity or personality,[58] which probably includes the right to make some personal facts public just as surely as it includes the right to keep some personal facts private.

The strength of the privacy or confidentiality interests involved. As Lord Hope recognised in *Campbell*, there are 'different degrees of privacy'.[59] The law reflects that in various ways. On the one hand, there are distinctions between personal privacy interests (protected by Article 8), purely commercial interests (such as trade secrets), and government secrets. Within those categories, there is in each case a hierarchy of interests—from the most intimate detail about a person's sexual life or health to mundane information about his address or taste in furniture, from secret formulae to information about customer preferences, from information about the identity of a secret agent, to information about who sits where at the cabinet table.[60] In striking a proper balance, this continuum (and fine gradations within it) has to be considered. Thus, for instance, greater

present to justify publication on this ground. But he seems to have agreed with the judge that the identification of some minor hypocrisy is not enough. Probably it depends on how the balance is struck, which must vary from case to case.

[54] *X & Y v Persons Unknown* [2006] EWHC 2783 (QB), [2007] HRLR 4, [28] (Eady J).

[55] *Ibid*, [27] (Eady J).

[56] *Ibid*, [28] (Eady J).

[57] *A v B plc* [2002] EWCA Civ 337, [2003] QB 195.

[58] Thus, for instance, Art 8 includes the right to have access to some information about one's identity and background (*Gaskin v United Kingdom* (1990) 12 EHRR 36), and the right to express one's sexual identity (*Dudgeon v United Kingdom* (1981) 4 EHRR 149), and the right to present oneself publicly with a particular gender identity (*B v France* (1992) 16 EHRR 1; *Goodwin v United Kingdom* (2002) 35 EHRR 447). It seems clear, therefore, that Art 8 includes not only the right to keep some things hidden from the public, but also to know, act upon and share with others important aspects of one's personality.

[59] [2004] UKHL 22, [2004] 2 AC 457, [118].

[60] See the quotation from *R v Shayler*, text to n 17 above.

solicitude will be shown for information about long-term relationships such as marriage than for transitory sexual encounters.[61] Greater weight attaches to the maintenance of confidentiality where that has been agreed, than to cases between strangers.[62] By contrast, the continued secrecy of a report about which there is no 'genuine commercial sensitivity' was easily outweighed by the public interest in understanding the bidding process leading to the award of major public contract.[63]

The nature and degree of detriment which will be suffered by the claimant (or third parties) if disclosure takes place. This factor is obviously closely related to the previous one, and is in one sense an aspect of it. It has proved particularly important in cases involving government secrets, where the courts generally decline to prevent publication unless some detriment can be shown.[64] Where the case does not concern government secrets, the position may be different,[65] but the nature and degree of any detriment to which the claimant or third parties (such as other family members or employees) would be exposed by publication must surely remain relevant and important.[66] It is likely to be particularly important where the claimant is vulnerable because of youth or mental illness.[67]

Relevant privacy codes. The Human Rights Act 1998 requires that, in cases concerning 'journalistic, literary or artistic material' the court should have 'particular regard' to any 'relevant privacy code'.[68] There is no definition of 'privacy code'. It certainly includes public codes such as that maintained by the Press Complaints Commission.[69] But the expression is arguably wide enough to extend to internal codes maintained by particular broadcasters or newspapers too.[70] As things stand, however, the value of these documents is limited. The codes themselves tend to be very broadly framed (the Press Complaints Commission code, for example, in its 2007 revision, does little more than restate the principle that the public interest is an exception to privacy, and identify certain well-established examples). More assistance might be derived from decisions of the Press Complaints Commission; but as things stand their citation is discouraged.[71]

[61] *A v B plc* [2002] EWCA Civ 337, [2003] QB 195, [47].

[62] *HRH Prince of Wales v Associated Newspapers Ltd* [2006] EWCA Civ 1776, [2007] 3 WLR 222.

[63] *London Regional Transport v The Mayor of London* [2001] EWCA Civ. 1491, [2003] EMLR 4.

[64] *Attorney-General v Jonathan Cape Ltd* [1976] QB 752; *Attorney-General v Guardian Newspapers Ltd (No 2)* [1991] 1 AC 109, 283 (Lord Goff).

[65] See below, p 147.

[66] For instance, if publication gives rise to a risk of physical injury: *Venables v News Group Newspapers Ltd* [2001] Fam 430.

[67] See, eg, *Venables v News Group Newspapers Ltd* [2001] Fam 430; *X (a woman formerly known as Mary Bell) v News Group Newspapers Ltd* [2003] EWHC 1101 (QB), [2003] EMLR 37.

[68] Human Rights Act 1998, s 12 (4).

[69] *A v B plc* [2001] 1 WLR 2341, [22] (Jack J).

[70] Thus Tugendhat & Christie, 417.

[71] *A v B plc* [2002] EWCA Civ 337, [2003] QB 195, [11] (Lord Woolf MR).

§ 18

Protection of Legitimate Commercial Interests

(1) Subject to §§ 9–17, and to paragraph (2), information is protected even if its disclosure is necessary for the protection of the defendant's commercial interests.

(2) Where the claimant and defendant are in a contractual relationship (or a consensual relationship akin to contract), disclosure or use of information will be impliedly permitted where that is necessary to give business efficacy to the contract or relationship.

THIS SECTION ADDRESSES a potentially difficult issue. There is a line of cases, beginning with *Tournier v National Provincial and Union Bank of England*, recognising an exception to a duty of confidence where disclosure is required 'in the interests of' the confidant.[1] The principle has since been applied rarely in banking cases,[2] and has also surfaced in cases concerning arbitration proceedings,[3] where it has been framed as a right to use confidential information where that is 'reasonably necessary for the protection of the legitimate interests of the arbitrating party'.[4]

But, although the exception has received formal recognition in these cases, it has not proved particularly fruitful. The question has to be asked: Is it sound, in principle, as a general exception? With respect, it is suggested, it is not. It seems clear that a person may be under an obligation to keep information confidential even when it is very much contrary to her interests to do so. If for example, *A* were to receive, unsolicited, copies of some plans for a new machine to be manufactured by a competitor, *B*, it seems plain that it is *A*'s duty not to use those plans even if the invention in question would be so successful that it would drive

[1] [1924] 1 KB 461 (CA), 473 (Bankes LJ).

[2] *Sunderland v Barclays Bank Ltd* (1938) 5 *Legal Decisions Affecting Bankers* 163.

[3] *Ali Shipping Corp v Shipyard Trogir* [1999] 1 WLR 314 (CA); *Insurance Co v Lloyd's Syndicate* [1995] 1 Lloyd's Rep 272; *Hassneh Insurance Co of Israel v Mew* [1993] 2 Lloyd's Rep 243.

[4] *Ali Shipping Corp v Shipyard Trogir* [1999] 1 WLR 314 (CA), 327 (Potter LJ). Cf Brennan J's formulation in *Esso Australia Resources Ltd v Plowman* (1995) 183 CLR 10, 36: 'fairly required for the protection of a party's legitimate interests'.

A out of business. Similarly, a lawyer who receives confidential and privileged information from the other side in a case, and appreciates that a mistake has been made, is under a clear obligation to return the information unread and unused, even though it would be very much in his client's commercial interest to use it.[5] Even if full weight is given to the word 'necessary' in Potter LJ's formulation, it still seems too wide (and would certainly be too wide in any Article 8 case).

For these reasons, it is suggested, the proposition that there is always as a matter of law an exception or qualification for 'commercial interests' is to be rejected. The true position, it is suggested, is (*a*) that many cases where a person is protecting legitimate commercial interests will be handled under one of the preceding exceptions (§§ 9–17), and (*b*) that there may be other specific and limited exceptions in particular cases.

As to the first point, many cases of 'self-protection' can be more appropriately brought under one of the other recognised exceptions. A person who is under a legal obligation to disclose information can do so. It is in his interest to do so (to avoid whatever penalty attaches to breach of the obligation); but that is not the reason for the exception. Information, even confidential information, may be disclosed where it is necessary for the fair administration of justice. Where the case in question concerns confidant and confider, that will be in the confidant's interest;[6] but that is not the reason for the exception. An employee cannot be prevented from exercising his skills after the employment relationship ends,[7] and that is undoubtedly very much in the employee's interest. But it is not the reason for the exception, which rests on the public interest. In none of these cases is a separate exception needed.

Nevertheless, there may be cases where some limited further exception is required. The main aspects of such cases, it is suggested, are that they all stem from situations in which the confidentiality *does* rest on a consensual relationship, and are best understood not as reflections of some general exception, but rather as specific characteristics of the particular 'expectation of confidence' within such a relationship.

Take the example of the exception given in *Tournier*. If a banker sues a customer, she is permitted to disclose the amount the customer owes. That must be correct. It is a matter of necessary implication, given the very terms of the relationship which establishes the confidence. Without such a term, the contract could not work. In the same way, parties to an arbitration must be free to disclose the award if it is necessary to do so for the purposes of enforcement. Without such a liberty, the entire commercial arrangement would be unworkable.[8] In these

[5] *English & American Insurance Co v Herbert Smith* [1988] FSR 232.

[6] For instance, where a solicitor is sued by a client: see p 50 above, or where a doctor is sued by a patient: *Duncan v Medical Practitioners Disciplinary Committee* [1986] 1 NZLR 513, 521 (Jeffries J).

[7] See above, § 16.

[8] *Associated Electric and Gas Insurance Services v European Reinsurance Co of Zurich* [2003] UKPC 11, [2003] 1 WLR 1041.

cases, the exception being applied is not nearly as broad as the exception posited by Potter LJ. Indeed, it is not truly an exception at all, but rather a reflection of the limits of the confidentiality that the parties can be objectively taken to have agreed to.

§ 19

Change of Position

(1) Subject to paragraphs (2) and (3), a defendant is not relieved of a duty of confidence by the fact that he paid for the information, and did so in good faith.
(2) If the claimant seeks an account of profits, an allowance may be made for expenditure incurred and (provided the defendant acted in good faith) for the defendant's time and skill.
(3) In exceptional cases, an injunction (and, possibly, an account of profits) may be refused where it would cause hardship to the defendant.

THE QUESTION ADDRESSED in § 19 is one of very great uncertainty. There are a few dicta bearing on the questions here, and a certain amount of academic commentary. But there is no really decisive case, and the issues are not straightforward.

NO DEFENCE OF BONA-FIDE PURCHASE

It is clear, of course, that those who have not agreed to keep information confidential and have no notice (in any sense) that information is confidential are not liable for the use of that information so long as they remain ignorant. But once they obtain such notice, they will generally speaking be bound from that moment onwards, by a duty of confidence.[1] It has, however, occasionally been suggested that a person who *acquires* information in good faith might thereafter be left free to use it, even if she *subsequently* learns that it was confidential. In *Morison v Moat* when enforcing a duty of confidence against a third-party recipient of confidential information, Sir James Turner V-C said that the result:

> might be different if the defendant was a purchaser for value of the secret without notice of any obligation affecting it.[2]

[1] § 5. See, eg, *Valeo Vision Ltd v Flexible Lamps Ltd* [1995] RPC 205.
[2] (1851) 9 Hare 241, 263.

But so far as can be seen, the defence has never been applied. It has been explicitly rejected both in England[3] and Australia.[4] And it has generally met academic disapproval.[5]

There are two problems. As a technical matter, the defence of 'bona fide purchase' fastens on property: it protects the good-faith purchaser of a legal property interest against equitable interference with her legal rights. But information is not property.[6] As a result, reference to the 'bona fide purchaser' of information is 'merely a loose description of a person who pays money for the supply of information in ignorance that it is being supplied in breach of another's confidence.'[7] It is a sloppy and vague expression, ill-fitted to do sensible work as a defence. As a substantive matter, it is not clear why a person who happens to pay something (no matter how little) for information should by that fact be entirely relieved of any obligations if it subsequently transpires that the information was confidential. It would be 'somewhat shocking'[8] if such a person persisted in plans to use the information once the truth was discovered.

The better view therefore is that a duty of confidence will be enforced even against a person who paid, in good faith, for the information. The mere fact of good faith payment is not a complete answer.

A CHANGE OF POSITION DEFENCE?

Bona fide purchase, then, is not a complete defence. But does it follow that one should entirely ignore the fact that a defendant has paid for information, and perhaps spent money in the expectation of using it, and is now expected to sacrifice that outlay because of the claimant's confidentiality rights, newly discovered? Jones puts the following case:

> *D*, a business man, pays *R* for certain information which, unknown to *D*, *R* has imparted to *D* in breach of *P*'s confidence. *D* begins to develop a grip, using this information. His expenditure of plant, machinery and leasehold premises has been very substantial. *D* is then told by *P*, who has just discovered *R*'s duplicity, the true facts. Three years have elapsed since he paid *R* for the information.[9]

[3] At first instance in *Stephenson Jordan & Harrison Ltd v MacDonald & Evans* (1951) 68 RPC 190, reversed on other grounds (1952) 69 RPC 10. There are dicta of Nourse LJ in *Spycatcher* (see [1990] 1 AC 109, 177, where they are quoted with apparent approval by Lord Donaldson MR) which might be taken to support such a defence: see Toulson & Phipps, para 3–057. But on closer inspection those dicta appear rather to support the proposition that a third party recipient of confidential information is *always* bound by a duty of confidence unless he is a bona-fide purchaser for value without notice. As such they are clearly too wide, since a person who does not have notice of confidentiality is not subject to any duty, even if she is a volunteer: see § 5.

[4] *Wheatley v Bell* [1984] FSR 16.

[5] See Toulson & Phipps, para 3–057.

[6] See App B.

[7] Toulson & Phipps, para 3–061.

[8] *Stephenson Jordan & Harrison Ltd v MacDonald & Evans* (1952) 69 RPC 10 (CA), 16 (Lord Evershed MR).

[9] G Jones, 'Restitution of Benefits Obtained in Breach of Another's Confidence' (1970) 86 *LQR* 463, 479.

Intuitively, *D* seems to have a stronger claim to some sort of defence in these circumstances. But of what sort?

Perhaps, as Toulson and Phipps and Professor Jones suggest, the answer lies in the defence of 'change of position': *D* should have a partial defence to the extent that he has changed his position by spending money in reliance on his perceived entitlement to use the information. It is suggested, however, that such a conclusion requires rather careful analysis, and that upon analysis it turns out to be too simple. In order to unpick the position, it is necessary to look separately at each of the main remedies a claimant in a breach of confidence case might seek: an account of profits, damages as compensation for loss, and an injunction to restrain further misuse of the information.

A claim for an account of profits is a restitutionary remedy: it seeks to transfer from the defendant to the claimant a sum that represents the defendant's gain (not the claimant's loss). In relation to a breach of confidence, it is a restitutionary claim based on a wrong done by the defendant to the claimant. As such it is probable that the change of position defence recognised by the House of Lords in *Lipkin Gorman v Karpnale Ltd*[10] would be available.[11] But would it be needed? When an account is taken all just allowances will be made.[12] That would naturally include the costs incurred in making the profits, so that 'any change of position will inevitable reflect itself as a debit item in the account of profits'.[13] It may indeed go further since, provided the accounting party acted in good faith, an allowance may be made for that party's contribution in skill and effort in obtaining the profit.[14] Given those allowances, it seems hard to imagine any circumstances in which a change of position defence would serve any useful function in relation to an account of profits. Nevertheless, it is conceivable that a court might regard an account of profits as unfairly harsh where the defendant had acted in good faith, and to this extent a defence somewhat similar to change of position may exist.[15] But it is not a true change of position defence, since it does not operate *pro tanto*, but as a complete bar to a particular remedy, and it is discretionary.

A claim for damages is not restitutionary, but compensatory. It is hard to identify any legitimate principle upon which a defence of change of position—which is a defence to restitutionary claims—could be applied to reduce

[10] [1991] 2 AC 548 (HL).

[11] Likely but not certain, because of residual doubt about whether the defence applies to restitution for wrongs, given Lord Goff's comment at [1991] 2 AC 548, 580, that the defence should not be open to a 'wrongdoer'. For discussion see A Burrows, *The Law of Restitution,* 2nd edn (London, 2002), 524–7.

[12] CPR Pt 40 PD, [4]. See further § 24, below.

[13] G Jones, 'Restitution of Benefits Obtained in Breach of Another's Confidence' (1970) 86 *LQR* 463, 478.

[14] *Boardman v Phipps* [1967] 2 AC 46 (HL).

[15] This appears to have been the view of the Court of Appeal in *Seager v Copydex Ltd* [1967] 1 WLR 923. In *Satnam Investments Ltd v Dunlop Heywood & Co Ltd* [1999] 3 All ER 652 (CA), an account of profits was refused on grounds that it would be disproportionate.

damages.[16] Nor does there seem to be any reason why it should be. If the defendant, by using confidential information with notice of its confidentiality, has caused loss to the claimant, the 'equities' do not seem likely in any conceivable situation to favour requiring the *claimant* to make some sort of counter-compensation for loss suffered by the defendant.

Finally, there is the claim for an injunction. That is neither restitutionary nor compensatory. It is a remedy that seeks directly to vindicate the claimant's rights and to prevent both loss and unjust enrichment. The change of position defence recognised in *Lipkin Gorman* cannot apply, since it is a partial defence to a money claim (that is, it absolves the defendant from making restitution *but only to the extent that* the defendant has changed his position). But the injunction is necessarily an all-or-nothing remedy: either an injunction is granted, or it is refused.

Here there are two possibilities, however. An injunction is a discretionary remedy, and (on established principles) the court:

> may decline to grant an injunction if to do so will result in such substantial hardship to the defendant that . . . disproportionate prejudice will be caused by its intervention.[17]

Closely related to this principle is the doctrine that equity may impose, as a pre-condition on granting relief, a requirement that the claimant do something to prevent unfairness or harshness. Applying the maxim that 'he who seeks equity must do equity', relief may be made conditional upon the claimant meeting the defendant's expenses in certain respects.[18] In an appropriate case the court might use these doctrines to achieve fairness. For instance, if the claimant would suffer only a small degree of prejudice by the breach of confidence, whereas the defendant had in good faith spent very large sums in the anticipation of using the information, an injunction might conceivably be refused, or granted only on terms that the claimant compensate the defendant for his lost expenditure.

Thus there do seem to be such cases, where the loss liable to be suffered by a defendant who has invested largely and in good faith by the grant of an injunction warrants its refusal.[19] But they are likely to be rare. In the first place, it is not as a general matter by any means clear that in an example such as that given by Jones,[20] the 'equities' really favour *D*. Both *P* and *D* are innocent victims of *R*. *P* has done nothing to encourage *D* to make the expenditure in question, and was not even aware of it. Nor has *P* benefited from it. In those circumstances

[16] See A Burrows, *The Law of Restitution,* 2nd edn (London, 2002) 524: 'Clearly change of position is irrelevant to compensation for wrongs'.

[17] ICF Spry, *Equitable Remedies,* 7th edn (Pymont, 2001) 400.

[18] See, eg, *Ramsden v Dyson* (1866) LR1HL129; *Re Berkeley Applegate (Investment Consultants) Ltd* [1989] Ch 32.

[19] See, eg, *Seager v Copydex Ltd* [1967] 1 WLR 923 (CA), and the comments of Megarry J in *Coco v AN Clark (Engineers) Ltd* [1969] RPC 41, 49–50, distinguishing a duty not to use information and a duty not to use it without payment.

[20] Text to n 9 above.

there does not, as a general matter seem to be any respect in which it could be said to be unconscionable for *P* to insist on his rights without compensating *D*. If *D* has a complaint, it is against *R*. That is not to say that there might never be rare cases in which the position was different, where the hardship to *D* was utterly disproportionate to the damage to *P*. But it would require such a case, and not merely *some* sort of change of position on *D*'s part, to justify taking such an approach.

Part III

Remedies and Procedure

§ 20

Parties

(1) The following are proper claimants in an action for breach of confidence—

(a) a person to whom the relevant duty of confidence was owed, or
(b) the assignee of such a person.

(2) The following are liable as defendants to an action alleging breach of confidence—

(a) a person who owed a duty of confidence and misused protected information;
(b) a person who participated in a common design or plan to misuse protected information; or
(c) a person who knowingly induced or procured a third party to misuse protected information.

(3) Exceptionally, an injunction may be granted although no defendant can be identified.

CLAIMANTS: DIRECT CLAIMANTS

THERE IS NO real mystery to identifying the proper claimant or claimants to an action for breach of confidence. The primary work is done by the rules set out in §§ 1 and 2: the proper claimant in any case is the person who had a reasonable expectation of confidence, the 'party who is entitled to the confidence and to have it respected'.[1] That is not the same thing, of course, as having access to the information. In *Fraser v Evans*[2] the claimant was privy to the information, but he had no expectation of confidentiality in it. It was held he had no title to sue.

Just as not everyone who is privy to the information is owed any duty of confidence, so a person may be owed a duty of confidence even in respect of information that he does not know or have access to. At first this seems

[1] *Fraser v Evans* [1969] 1 QB 349 (CA), 361 (Lord Denning MR).
[2] *Ibid.*

counterintuitive. But there is no reason in principle why a person should not have an expectation of confidentiality in information she does not yet know, and may not even be entitled to learn. If you take a photograph of me in a private place, I have no right to see that photograph, but it may well be confidential to me. Similarly, in *Douglas v Hello Ltd! (No 3)*,[3] OK! magazine as the chosen publisher of an exclusive story about the Douglases' wedding was owed a duty of confidence in relation to photographic information about the wedding, even though it had no positive right to obtain any such photographs. This is as it should be, for confidentiality is about what is kept secret, not what is known.

More than one person may have a reasonable expectation of confidence in relation to any given piece of information. Thus, in *Douglas*,[4] both Michael Douglas and Catherine Zeta-Jones had personal interests in the privacy of their wedding photographs, and OK! magazine also had a commercial expectation of confidentiality. And in a number of cases it has been accepted that a hospital has its own expectation that employees will maintain the confidentiality of patient files, which entitles the hospital to take action to protect them;[5] there seems to be no doubt that individual patients could also have taken action to protect their medical records. A similar approach would be taken to other professionals, if confidential information relating to clients were to be extracted from their files. Where several people participate in an economic venture, information may be confidential to all of them.[6] In such cases the claimant, in protecting her own interests, may also in practice protect the interests of others. But the action is taken not merely as a representative, but in order to enforce the claimant's own rights in respect of information over which others, too, have rights. In principle, absent some special factor, a private law claimant must be the person to whom the duty of confidence is owed.[7]

Is it necessary, where there are multiple persons owed duties of confidentiality in respect of the same information, that all should be joined as parties? One case suggests that it may be.[8] But the balance of authority is against the proposition.[9] Unless the remedy being sought includes an account of profits there seems to be no reason why a single claimant should not suffice, since the interest protected is separate not joint.

[3] [2007] UKHL 21, [2007] 2 WLR 920.

[4] *Ibid.*

[5] *Ashworth Security Hospital v MGN Ltd* [2002] UKHL 29, [2002] 1 WLR 2033, [32] Lord Woolf; *Mersey Care NHS Trust v Ackroyd* [2006] EWHC 17 (QB), affirmed [2007] EWCA Civ 101; *Green Corns Ltd v Claverley Group Ltd* [2005] EWHC 958 (QB), [2005] EMLR 31. In *Ackroyd* [2006] EWHC 17, [96], Tugendhat J stressed that the hospital did not sue on behalf of its patients.

[6] *Gilbert v Star Newspaper Ltd* (1894) 11 TLR 4. It is a separate question whether, if one of the participants leaves the venture, he is able to prevent the remaining participants using the information as they see fit: see *Murray v Yorkshire Fund Managers Ltd* [1998] 1 WLR 951 (CA).

[7] Of course, where the claimant is a minor or incapacitated arrangements for representation may have to be made. This does not affect the basic principle.

[8] *Gilbert v Star Newspaper Ltd* (1894) 11 TLR 4, where proceedings were adjourned for the joinder of a person with such an interest.

[9] See, in particular, those cases cited at n 5, where the hospital was able to act to enforce its own confidentiality rights without joining the patients who had rights in relation to the same information.

Where there are multiple claimants, each with a separate interest, the remedies granted may need to be carefully considered. There is no fundamental difficulty with damages: each claimant ought to be able to recover her own loss.[10] Nor does there appear to be a difficulty with the grant of an injunction: in principle either claimant ought to be able to obtain an injunction (if it is appropriate). There could, however, be difficulties with accounts of profits. The defendant would obviously only have to account once, and the profits in question would have to be divided between claimants in some way. That would be a reason to insist on having all possible claimants before the court. There would be a risk, otherwise, that a defendant might be obliged to account to the claimant in one action, and then find himself sued in a fresh action by a different claimant. If one claimant sought an account, and the others damages, a choice would have to be made (since the remedies are incompatible). It is suggested that, in such a case, the court would probably refuse to order an account of profits unless all claimants were agreed on that remedy.[11]

ASSIGNMENTS

Two separate situations should be distinguished. The first is that of assignment, properly so called. There are cases where the claimant has the benefit of an express assignment, either of contractual rights (including express or implied confidentiality rights) or of equitable rights.[12] It seems probable that purely personal rights (such as those between spouses) are not properly the object of an assignment;[13] but there seems no reason why commercial rights associated with trade secrets and the like should not be transferred by assignment.[14] There seems to be nothing objectionable about enforcing such an assignment in the ordinary way, the assignee standing in the shoes of the assignor. (But, where the rights assigned are contractual, it would normally be necessary to join the assignor as a party, the assignment being equitable.[15])

[10] As happened, for instance, in *Douglas v Hello! Ltd (No 3)* [2007] UKHL 21, [2007] 2 WLR 920: the Douglases recovered a small sum for their non-financial losses, and OK! Ltd recovered a much larger sum for its financial loss.

[11] See *Spring Form Inc v Toy Brokers Ltd* [2002] FSR 17, 288 (Pumfrey J). Though the decision there was assisted by the statutory provisions at issue, it seems right in any event as a matter of principle.

[12] This was the position in *O Mustad & Son v Dosen* (1928), *Note* [1964] 1 WLR 109 (HL). It is not apparent from the report of the House of Lords' decision, but is apparent from the judgments of the Court of Appeal and the pleadings, available in Lincoln's Inn Library.

[13] See Tugendhat & Christie, para 6.140.

[14] In *Douglas v Hello Ltd (No 3)*, the Court of Appeal treated the Douglases' rights as capable of transfer, albeit not actually transferred. In the House of Lords, Lord Hoffman at least hinted that the *personal* rights as non-assignable, resting his decision on the existence of commercial rights: [2007] UKHL 21, [2007] 2 WLR 920, [118]. The view that personal privacy rights are not assignable in equity is shared by Meagher, Gummow & Lehane, para 41-070.

[15] *Three Rivers District Council v Governor and Company of the Bank of England* [1996] QB 292 (CA). For an equitable assignment of equitable rights, no joinder would be necessary.

The more difficult case is that of 'assignment' or transfer 'of the information' used in a loose sense, that is where *A*, having confidential information, agrees to 'sell' it to *B*. Since information is not property, what is the effect of such a transaction? The answer, it is suggested, is that provided the 'sale' is appropriately structured, *B* will normally acquire a free-standing and independent expectation of confidentiality in her own right. It will normally be an incident of such a sale that *A* agrees not to use the information, or to pass it to others. In effect, from that point onwards, *B* will have her own expectation of confidentiality, which can be enforced. But that consequence does not flow primarily from the fact that *A* has shared the *benefit* of the information with *B*. If *A* provided the information to *B* on terms which left *A* free to provide the same information to others, *B*'s confidentiality rights would be qualified or avoided, simply because *B* could not realistically claim to have any expectation of confidentiality.[16] What really matters is that *A* and *B* have, by the terms of their dealing with each other and with the information, established a structure within which the information has become confidential to *B*. No special doctrine of 'assignment' is required to deal with these cases, and *B* ought to be free to enforce her own rights of confidence.

DEATH

There is no doubt that pre-existing causes of action for breach of a duty of confidence survive death, and transfer to the estate.[17] But what of the duties themselves? The question is undecided. It seems likely that some sorts of duty of confidence (relating, for instance, to trade secrets) may be regarded as passing with the estate, so that they are treated as part of the assets of the estate.[18] Others are controversial. For instance, it is an unresolved question whether personal privacy rights survive death, and if so for how long.[19]

DEFENDANTS: PRIMARY MISUSERS

Just as the appropriate group of claimants is normally circumscribed by §§ 1 and 2, so the proper defendants are normally identified by §§ 4, 5 and 6: they are those who, having agreed to or with notice of the claimant's expectation of confidentiality nevertheless misuse the information, or threaten to do so. There may, of course, be more than one such person. If a jilted lover goes to the press which publishes a story, both the lover and the newspaper will be liable: both owe duties of confidence, and both have misused the confidential information.

[16] For instance, if *A* sells a confidential story to *B* newspaper but on a non-exclusive basis

[17] Law Reform (Miscellaneous Provisions) Act 1934, s 1.

[18] See, by analogy, *Green v Folgham* (1823) 1 Sim & St 398.

[19] In *Gunn-Russo v Nugent Care Society* [2001] EWHC Admin 566, [2002] 2 FLR 1, [51], Scott Baker J thought that they could survive death. The same view is taken by the GMC and the Law Society in relation to client confidences.

Such multiple or successive misuse does not necessarily render each defendant jointly liable for a single wrong. It will do so if all the wrongful acts occur pursuant to a common design; but where each defendant acts independently, each is separately and severally liable, even if (as may be the case) their liability in damages would be co-extensive.

ACCESSORIES

A defendant may also be held liable (as a joint wrongdoer) where she has participated in a joint plan with another defendant which involves the misuse of confidential information. Joint liability in tort attaches to:

> two persons who agree on common action, in the course of, and to further which, one of them commits a tort.[20]

The principle applies to breaches of intellectual property rights.[21] There seems to be no reason why it should not be applied to participants in a common design that involves a breach of confidence.

Accessory liability also attaches to those who induce or procure others to commit torts,[22] or knowingly induce breaches of contract.[23] There seems no good reason in principle why the knowing inducement of a person to breach a confidence should not also be wrongful.[24] For reasons explained in § 5, however, the common situation in which one person wrongfully provides information to another, and the second then uses or discloses that information, is not properly to be regarded as a case of accessory liability (the second wrongdoer being liable *for* the first wrong), but as a case where each discloser breaches an independent duty of confidence.

JOHN DOE INJUNCTIONS AND INJUNCTIONS *CONTRA MUNDUM*

In the normal way, the claimant is expected to identify the defendant to any action by name, and any order granted is made against the identified defendant. Sometimes, however, this ordinary practice is relaxed, and relief can be sought and obtained without identifying the defendant.

[20] *The Koursk* [1924] P 140 (CA), 155 (Scrutton LJ). See also *Brooke v Bool* [1928] 2 KB 578 (DC).

[21] *CBS Songs Ltd v Amstrad Consumer Electronics plc* [1988] AC 1013 (HL), 1056, 1057 ('two or more persons who act in concert with one another pursuant to a common design in the infringement') (Lord Templeman). In that case, however, there was no common design. See also *Unilever plc v Gilette (UK) Ltd* [1989] RPC 583 (CA), 603 (Mustill LJ).

[22] *Allen v Flood* [1898] AC 1 (HL), 96 (Lord Watson).

[23] *OBG Ltd v Allan* [2007] 21 UKHL.

[24] The only difficulty would be with the Court of Appeal's conclusion, in *Metall und Rohstoff AG v Donaldson Lufkin & Jenrette Inc* [1990] 1 QB 391 (CA), 481, that it is not a tort to induce a breach of trust. But the CA seems to have accepted that it could be a wrong to induce a breach of other equitable obligations, and in particular breach of confidence. Their comments were restricted to claims to induce a breach of trust, as such, and not to other equitable wrongs.

There are two separate categories of case. The first is where the defendant's name is unknown. In *Bloomsbury Publishing Ltd v News Group Newspapers Ltd*[25] several copies of the (then unpublished) novel *Harry Potter and the Order of the Phoenix* were stolen from the printers. The publishers became aware that someone was offering them for sale to the press, but could not establish that person's identity (or the identity of all of the people involved). Sir Andrew Morritt V-C held that proceedings could be brought and an order made against persons unknown. In *X & Y v Persons Unknown*[26] Eady J granted an injunction against an unknown person who was believed to be offering information about the claimants' marital difficulties for sale to newspapers. The true 'targets' of such injunctions are, of course, the newspapers who will be notified of the order.[27]

The main difficulties that arise with such injunctions concern the description of the defendants, and service upon them (both of the proceedings and the order). In both *Bloomsbury Publishing Ltd* and *X & Y* the defendants were identified based on their activities, as the persons or 'who have offered' or 'who have provided' specified information to newspapers. The description should be clear and objective, as it was in those cases, and 'sufficiently certain as to identify both those who are included and those who are not'.[28] It should not involve any reference to contentious legal issues,[29] nor should it identify them by reference to their subjective states of mind.[30] So an action against a person 'breaching confidence' or 'proposing to offer' would be inappropriate.

The second question concerns service. Although the main objective will generally be to notify newspapers, proceedings must in some way be served on the defendant. This was not discussed in *Bloomsbury*. In *X & Y* a number of possible approaches were canvassed—directing that attempts be made to trace the persons concerned, serving all the likely candidates, attempting to obtain disclosure of their identity through orders directed against newspapers, or substituted service by some alternative method.[31] The proper approach must be tailored to the particular case. But it is clear that the claimant cannot be permitted simply to obtain the injunction and then neglect service (otherwise an interim injunction becomes de facto permanent).[32]

A different (and in some ways more startling procedure) involves the making of an *order* 'against the world' (*contra mundum*). This practice is discussed in

[25] [2003] EWHC 1205 (Ch), [2003] 1 WLR 1633.

[26] [2006] EWHC 2783 (QB), [2007] HRLR 4.

[27] Once notified they will be entitled to apply to discharge or vary it. It is good practice, in most cases, to notify them in advance of the application so that they can appear and make submissions: *X & Y v Persons Unknown*, [2006] EWHC 2783 (QB), [2007] HRLR 4, [18] (Eady J).

[28] *Bloomsbury Publishing Ltd v News Group Newspapers Ltd* [2003] EWHC 1205 (Ch), [2003] 1 WLR 1633, [21] (Morritt V-C).

[29] *Hampshire Waste Services Ltd v Persons Intending to Trespass* [2003] EWHC 1738 (Ch), [2004] Env LR 9, [9] (Morritt V-C).

[30] *Ibid* [9] (Morritt V-C) ('intending'); *South Cambridgeshire DC v Persons Unknown* [2004] EWCA Civ 1280, *The Times*, 11 Nov 2004 ('proposing').

[31] CPR 6.8.

[32] *X & Y v Persons Unknown* [2006] EWHC 2783 (QB), [2007] HRLR 4, [78] (Eady J).

more detail in § 21. So far as *parties* are concerned, the usual practice is to ensure that a selection of interested persons who might (loosely, not technically) represent those likely to oppose such an order—for instance, the media—are joined, and to give notice also to the Attorney-General so that the public interest can be represented.

§ 21

Final Injunctions

(1) A final prohibitory injunction will be granted as a matter of course to prevent continued or threatened misuse of protected information.
(2) In an appropriate case, mandatory orders will be made for the delivery up or destruction of documents recording protected information.

FINAL PROHIBITORY INJUCTIONS

INJUNCTIONS ARE GRANTED as a matter of course where the defendant is tortiously interfering with or threatens to interfere with proprietary rights,[1] or to breach a negative contractual obligation.[2] Although breach of confidence need not involve any interference with property or contractual rights, an injunction nevertheless lies, the court having:

> original and independent jurisdiction to prevent what [it] considered and treated as a wrong, whether arising from a violation of an unquestionable right or from breach of contract or confidence.[3]

It is thus the 'general rule . . . that the [c]ourt will restraint the improper or unfair use of confidential information'.[4] Although there are some judicial dicta suggesting that a final injunction might be refused simply because damages would be an adequate remedy,[5] the true practical position seems to be that a final (as opposed to an interim) injunction will be granted even where the court doubts that the claimant would suffer significant or uncompensable damage.[6]

[1] *Pride of Derby v British Celanese Ltd* [1953] Ch 149 (CA), 181 (Evershed MR); *Attorney-General v PYA Quarries Ltd* [1957] 2 QB 169 (CA), 188 (Romer LJ).

[2] *Doherty v Allman* (1878) LR 3 App Cas 709 (HL), 719–20 (Lord Cairns).

[3] *Pollard v Photographic Co* (1888) 40 Ch D 345, 354 (North J). See also *Attorney-General v Guardian Newspapers Ltd* (No 2) [1990] 1 AC 109, 224 (Bingham LJ), where *Pride of Derby v British Celanese Ltd* [1953] Ch 149 was treated as applicable to confidentiality claims.

[4] *AB Consolidated Ltd v Europe Strength Food Co Pty Ltd* [1978] 2 NZLR 515, 526 (Woodhouse J).

[5] *Attorney-General v Guardian Newspapers Ltd* (No 2) [1990] 1 AC 109 (HL), 218, Bingham LJ

[6] For an example, see the decision of Harman J in *Nichrotherm Electrical Co Ltd v Percy* [1956] RPC 272, affirmed [1957] RPC 207.

The court having decided that the claimant's equitable rights are being infringed, the injunction issues as a matter of course, since 'a person by committing a wrongful act . . . is not thereby entitled to ask the Court to sanction his doing so by purchasing his neighbour's rights, by assessing damages in that behalf.'[7]

Nevertheless, although granted 'as a matter of course', the injunction remains a discretionary remedy, and may be withheld in exceptional circumstances. In particular, a final injunction may be refused if it would cause quite disproportionate hardship to the defendant.[8] The discretion should be exercised to refuse an injunction where the claimant is responsible for some conduct or inaction (such as laches or acquiescence) which on normal principles would lead equity to refuse relief. But absent such special circumstances, a claimant who wishes to prevent continued breach of confidence by the defendant ought normally to be given the court's assistance.[9]

THE TERMS OF AN INJUNCTION: SPECIFICITY

As a matter of general principle, an injunction to restrain the misuse of confidential information 'ought to be such that the party affected can know with certainty what he is or is not allowed to do.'[10] An injunction which restrains the use of 'confidential information', without specifying *what* information is confidential will normally be inappropriately wide.[11] If the claimant is unable to describe the confidential information with sufficient specificity,[12] or the resulting injunction would be unworkable,[13] an injunction will be refused. If the injunction is vague or ambiguous it may be impossible to enforce.[14]

[7] *Shelfer v City of London* [1895] 1 Ch 287, 322 (AL Smith LJ), approved in this context by Lord Evershed MR in *Terrapin Ltd v Builders Supply Co (Hayes) Ltd* [1960] RPC 128 (CA), 135.

[8] See, eg, *Ocular Sciences Ltd v Aspect Vision Care Ltd* [1997] RPC 289, 406–7, where an injunction was refused; see also § 19 above.

[9] The cases suggest some additional emphasis on the exercise of discretion where the case involves an injunction to restrain the use of a confidential and privileged document disclosed by mistake: *Webster v James Chapman & Co* [1989] 3 All ER 939; *Istil Group Inc v Zahoor* [2003] EWHC 165 (Ch), [2003] 2 All ER 252; *Al Fayed v Commissioner of Police for the Metropolis* [2002] EWCA Civ 780, [16]. Such cases would be better explained as turning on the application of the public interest defence itself (§ 11), and in particular the public interest in the administration of justice (§ 14), rather than on the discretionary refusal of a remedy.

[10] *Potters-Ballotini Ltd v Weston-Baker* [1977] RPC 202 (CA), 206 (Lord Denning MR); *Times Newspapers Ltd v MGN Ltd* [1993] EMLR 443, 447 (Bingham MR). See also *Lord Browne of Madingley v Associated Newspapers Ltd* [2007] EWCA Civ 295, [2007] 3 WLR 289, [64]; *Lawrence David Ltd v Ashton* [1989] ICR 123 (CA), 132 (Balcombe LJ).

[11] *Intelsec Systems Ltd v Grech-Cini* [2000] 1 WLR 1190, 1209 (Nicholas Warren QC).

[12] *CMI Centers for Medical Innovation GmbH v Phytopharm plc* [1999] FSR 235, [45] (Laddie J).

[13] *Times Newspapers Ltd v MGN Ltd* [1993] EMLR 443 (CA); *Baker v Gibbons* [1972] 1 WLR 693, 702 (Pennycuick V-C).

[14] *PA Thomas & Co v Mould* [1968] 2 QB 913.

Beyond that, it is a matter of discretion for the judge granting the injunction to ensure that it is appropriately framed.[15] Particular care is needed where there is an overlap between information that is confidential and other information about the same or a similar topic that is not. It is common to include a 'public domain' proviso to orders restricting publication, in order to ensure that information on the relevant topic is not prevented from publication where it is already in the public domain.[16] But such a purely general proviso may not suffice. Where it is clear that some information *is* in the public domain, and it ought to be capable of specific identification, then an injunction may be refused if it is not identified. It should not simply be left to be identified later in the context of contempt proceedings.[17]

THE DURATION OF ANY INJUNCTION

A final injunction need not be perpetual. The information in question ought to be protected only so long as it remains confidential. So where, for instance, information is to be made publicly available at a later date, the injunction ought to apply only until the information is publicly available.[18] The question is most often important in so-called 'springboard' cases,[19] where the injunction is granted to prevent the defendant from obtaining an unfair advantage from misusing confidential information whose substance might be replicated, given sufficient time and trouble, from publicly available sources. In such cases, the injunction ought only to be granted for a period long enough to offset or prevent the unfair advantage.[20]

MANDATORY ORDERS: DESTRUCTION AND DELIVERY UP

If confidential information exists in physical form (for instance, as a paper record, or on electronic media, or even embodied in a physical object—as where a defendant has used confidential information to manufacture something), the court may order that the physical material be delivered up for destruction or destroyed. Such an order does not depend on the claimant being the owner of the material in question.[21] It is applied readily (almost, it is suggested, as a

[15] *Lord Browne of Madingley v Associated Newspapers Ltd* [2007] EWCA Civ 295, [2007] 3 WLR 289, [65].

[16] *X & Y v Persons Unknown* [2006] EWHC 2783 (QB), [2007] HRLR 4.

[17] *CMI-Centers for Medical Innovation GmbH v Phytopharm plc* [1999] FSR 235, [45].

[18] See, *eg*, *Gilbert v Star Newspaper Co Ltd* (1894) 11 TLR 4.

[19] See p 41 above.

[20] *Roger Bullivant Ltd v Ellis* [1987] ICR 464 (CA), 476 (Neill LJ).

[21] A claimant who does own the physical material will, of course, be entitled to an order for its delivery—not for destruction, or because of the information it contains, but in vindication of property rights in the material itself.

matter of course) where the document or article containing the confidential information embodies *only* the confidential information, and is not inherently valuable—such as paper records of the confidential information, plans and drawings and the like.[22] Greater difficulty applies where the confidential information has become mixed with valuable information of the defendant's own, which could not be preserved separately, or where it is embodied in some article of real inherent value. But the courts show few tender feelings towards wrongdoers, particularly where they have acted with conscious fault. The mere fact that the documents also contain information confidential to the defendant is not a reason to refuse the order.[23] So far as physical items are concerned, if the article in question could never legitimately be used or sold by the defendant, because it involves such misuse of the claimant's information that this could not be permitted, and particularly where the defendant was a conscious wrongdoer, destruction will nevertheless be ordered.[24] But courts have been reluctant to make an order which would simply lead to the destruction of valuable or useful property or equipment.[25] It must, presumably, be a question of discretion in any case—taking into account the need to safeguard the claimant's rights, and whatever steps are realistically required to do so, but avoiding causing unreasonable or disproportionate harm to the defendants, particularly innocent defendants.

THE EFFECT OF FINAL INJUNCTIONS

It is a general principle that final injunctions bind only parties to litigation,[26] and ought to be drafted so as to make that clear.[27] In the case of *interim* injunctions this principle is, in effect, qualified by the rule that third parties who knowingly frustrate the objective an injunction was designed to achieve commit a contempt of court, even though they do not breach the injunction or cause or assist a party to do so.[28] But that principle applies only to conduct which interferes with the administration of justice in a pending case, and does not therefore apply to final injunctions.[29]

The principle that injunctions bind only the parties is subject to two qualifications—only one of which represents a true exception. An apparent exception

[22] *Prince Albert v Strange* (1849) 2 De G & S M 652, 716 (Knight-Bruce V-C) (the catalogues). Where the defendant claims to have destroyed all records, the court will readily require that to be verified on oath: *Intelsec Systems Ltd v Grech-Cini* [2000] 1 WLR 1190.

[23] *Industrial Furnaces Ltd v Reaves* [1970] RPC 605, 628 (Graham J).

[24] *Franklin v Giddins* [1978] Qd R 72 (cuttings improperly taken and propagated); *Peter Pan Manufacturing Corp v Corsets Silhouette Ltd* [1964] 1 WLR 96 (bras); *Reid & Sigrist Ltd v Moss & Mechanism Ltd* (1932) 49 RPC 461.

[25] *Saltman Engineering Co Ltd v Campbell Engineering Co Ltd* (1948) 65 RPC 203 (CA), 219.

[26] *Iveson v Harris* (1802) 7 Ves Jun 251, 256.

[27] *Marengo v Daily Sketch and Sunday Graphic Ltd* [1948] 1 All ER 406 (HL).

[28] *Attorney-General v Times Newspapers Ltd* [1992] 1 AC 191 (HL). See p __ below.

[29] *Jockey Club v Buffham* [2002] EWHC 1866 (QB), [2003] QB 462; *Attorney-General v Punch Ltd* [2001] EWCA Civ 403, [2001] QB 1028, [86]–[88] (Lord Phillips MR).

is *John Doe* injunctions—that is, injunctions against 'persons unknown' who are identified by description rather than name in the proceedings. These, however, are not true exceptions to that principle, since the 'persons unknown' *are* parties, and identified as such, albeit not by name.[30] The only true exception is the case of injunctions *contra mundum*. These are orders directed at the world at large, and thus a true exception to the principle that orders are made against and binding only upon parties to the litigation.

The main difficulty with the injunction *contra mundum* is that it has developed pragmatically, as a response to the perceived needs of justice in sensitive contexts. It first emerged in the context of the court's wardship jurisdiction,[31] and more or less remained in that context until the end of the twentieth century,[32] gradually expanding from its initial foothold in the court's protective jurisdiction over children to its jurisdiction over the mentally ill. Recently, however, those limitations seem to have been relaxed, so that *contra mundum* injunctions have come to be granted in cases where the claimant is not subject to the court's protective supervisory jurisdiction.[33] Most of the decided cases relate to circumstances where the perpetrators or participants of notorious crime have been given new identities.

The courts have, in all these cases, emphasised the 'exceptional' nature of the jurisdiction; and all the cases have involved evidence of a real risk of physical or psychological harm to the claimant from publication. Meanwhile, other cases have continued to point out that injunctions are generally granted *in personam* against persons who are parties to litigation, treating as heretical the proposition that a claimant who can show a breach of confidence has any right, in general, to relief against anyone other than the defendants who are parties to the action.[34] Outside the established area of the court's supervisory jurisdiction to protect the vulnerable, the injunction *contra mundum* is an innovation in search of a fully coherent principle or rationale.[35]

[30] See *Attorney-General v Newspaper Publishing plc* [1988] Ch 333 (CA), 369 (Donaldson MR).

[31] *Re X (A Minor) (Wardship: Injunction)* [1984] 1 WLR 1422.

[32] See the useful historical survey by Munby J in *Kelly v British Broadcasting Corp* [2001] Fam 59, 73–5. That the injunction was, in the mid-1990s, regarded as rooted in the court's power to safeguard those of whom it was exercising supervisory jurisdiction was made clear in *R v Central Independent Television plc* [1994] Fam 192.

[33] *Venables v News Group Newspapers Ltd* [2001] Fam 430; *X (a woman formerly known as Mary Bell) v News Group Newspapers Ltd* [2003] EWHC 1101, [2003] EMLR 37; *Carr v News Group Newspapers Ltd* [2005] EWHC 971; *Re KT* [2005] EWHC 3428 (Fam).

[34] *Jockey Club v Buffham* [2002] EWHC 1866 (QB), [2003] QB 462, [26] (Gray J).

[35] In *ibid*, [26], Gray J described it as an exercise of the court's 'prerogative jurisdiction'. It is not clear what he had in mind; with respect, the label 'prerogative' seems to serve simply to identify the jurisdiction as existing without any coherent statutory basis or warrant in common law precedent.

§ 22

Interim Injunctions

(1) An interim injunction may be granted to restrain conduct that the claimant alleges would be a misuse of protected information if it is in the interests of justice to do so.
(2) Where the defendant relies on a right of freedom of expression, no interim injunction will be granted unless the court is satisfied that the claimant is likely to establish at trial that publication should not be allowed.

THE GENERAL POSITION

IN THE COURSE of the *Spycatcher* saga, Sir John Donaldson MR vividly explained the importance of interim injunctions in confidentiality cases:

> Confidential information is like an ice cube. Give it to the party who undertakes to keep it in his refrigerator and you still have an ice cube by the time the matter comes to trial. Either party may then succeed in getting possession of the cube. Give it to the party who has no refrigerator or will not agree to keep it in one, and by the time of the trial you just have a pool of water which neither party wants. It is the inherently perishable nature of confidential information which gives rise to unique problems.[1]

Under section 37 of the Supreme Court Act 1981, an injunction (whether interim or final) can be granted in any case where it appears to the court to be 'just and convenient' to do so. Pursuant to that jurisdiction, the court may grant an injunction before trial to protect the position of the parties pending the determination of their legal rights. The general approach to the grant or refusal of such injunctions was established in *American Cyanamid Co v Ethicon Ltd*.[2] In particular, the court tries to avoid pre-judging the outcome of the case, aiming to arrive at a position which will be as fair as possible (or as little unfair as possible) to both parties, whichever way the matter is finally decided.

[1] *Attorney-General v Newspaper Publishing plc* [1988] Ch 333 (CA), 358.
[2] [1975] AC 396 (HL).

In the ordinary way, this means that the court does not attempt to decide, when granting or refusing an interim injunction, which party is likely to win. The claimant must, as a minimum, establish that the claim has a 'real prospect of success', or that there is a 'serious question to be tried'.[3] But this is not a high hurdle.[4] A variety of factors are then considered in a structured way: Would damages be an adequate remedy for the claimant? If so, no injunction is likely to be needed. Would the defendant, on the other hand, be adequately compensated by the award of damages for the loss caused by the injunction if the claim fails? If so, an injunction is likely to be appropriate. If *neither* party would be adequately compensated financially, then attention must turn to a variety of other factors, including the relative merits, under the rubric of the 'balance of convenience', if necessary falling back on the maintenance of the status quo (a principle which invariably provokes some debate as to what exactly *is* the status quo).

In breach of confidence cases it is often necessary to depart from this schema, for various reasons. It is helpful to consider the approach under a variety of headings: how the court looks at the merits, how it looks at the adequacy of damages to the claimant and the adequacy of compensation to the defendant, and the other facts, considered as part of the balance of convenience.

THE MERITS

As set out above, the general inclination in cases where an interim injunction is claimed is to avoid taking more than a cursory look at the merits. The claimant must establish only a 'real prospect of success'. But that is not an invariable rule, and in breach of confidence cases, it often does not apply.

Where rights of freedom of expression under Article 10 of the Convention are in issue, there is a statutory prohibition on the grant of an injunction to restrain publication before trial 'unless the court is satisfied that the applicant is likely to establish that publication should not be allowed.'[5] The meaning of 'likely' in this context has been controversial. In *Cream Holdings Ltd v Bannerjee*[6] the House of Lords decided that it does not always mean 'more likely than not'—it is a test which still permits a degree of flexibility. So, for example, if the application is very urgent (for instance, to hold the position in the very short term

[3] A variety of expressions were used in *American Cyanamid*, but in practice the 'real prospect of success' and 'serious question' expressions have been preferred over the apparently laxer requirement that the claim should not be 'frivolous': see *Mothercare Ltd v Robson Books Ltd* [1975] FSR 466, 474 (Megarry V-C). In *Attorney-General v Newspaper Publishing plc* [1988] Ch 333 (CA), 358, Donaldson MR referred to a 'case which is sufficiently plausible to be taken seriously'.

[4] *Alfred Dunhill Ltd v Sunoptic SA* [1979] FSR 337 (CA), 373 (Megaw LJ).

[5] Human Rights Act 1998, s 12 (3). S 12 (2) provides a procedural protection for freedom of expression by placing on a statutory footing the principle that no order should be made without notifying the respondent unless 'compelling reason' to the contrary exists. That is, however, the general rule for interim relief in any event: see CPR 23.4.

[6] [2004] UKHL 44, [2005] 1 AC 253.

while the parties prepare for a full hearing) or the potential harm very grave (for instance, of physical injury),[7] the court can grant an injunction even though it does not rate the claimant's odds of ultimate success as better than even. But, despite this flexibility, the requirement is fundamentally at odds with the notion that the court should in general refuse to consider the relative strengths of both parties' claims. Rather the reverse: if the defendant is seeking to exercise a right of free expression, the usual position is that the court should consider the relative strengths of both parties' claims. In a standard case, where an injunction is sought to prevent publication for a prolonged period up to trial of the action, and no exceptional circumstances exist, the hurdle is undoubtedly set higher than the ordinary *American Cyanamid* standard.[8]

Quite apart from the special statutory protection of freedom of expression, it is well-established that the merits of the parties' respective cases are relevant where the grant or refusal of an injunction will in effect decide the issue, so that no trial is likely to take place.[9] In many cases involving confidential information, that will be the position. If an employer is granted a 'springboard' injunction pending trial, for instance, it may very well be that by the time the trial takes place the 'springboard' period will in any event have expired.[10] And confidential information is often only of importance for a short period of time.[11] If it is not used promptly it may become so stale that it is never used or useful. In such cases, on perfectly ordinary principles, the relative merits have to be considered. In *Attorney-General v Times Newspapers Ltd* Lord Oliver went so far as to say that, in order to avoid injustice:

> it may be necessary for courts to balance the rights of the parties and to decide the issue . . . at the interlocutory stage on the prima facie merits and on the evidence then available.[12]

Moreover, because of the nature of confidential information, it often turns out that damages are a poor remedy for both parties. In those circumstances, even under *American Cyanamid* principles, the respective merits of the parties' cases would often be relevant, as a factor in the 'balance of convenience'. For all these reasons it is generally necessary, in a breach of confidence case, to do more than merely satisfy the court that the claimant's case is not far-fetched or hopeless.

[7] *Cream Holdings Ltd v Bannerjee* [2004] UKHL 44, [2005] 1 AC 245, [18] and [19] (Lord Nicholls). Such cases are no doubt rare, but see *Nicholls v British Broadcasting Corp* [1999] EMLR 791 (CA), where the risk was considered in relation to the identity of a police informer.

[8] *Cream Holdings Ltd v Bannerjee* [2004] UKHL 44, [2005] 1 AC 245, [20] (Lord Nicholls).

[9] *NWL Ltd v Woods* [1979] 1 WLR 1294 (HL), 1306 (Lord Diplock).

[10] *Lansing Linde Ltd v Kerr* [1991] 1 WLR 251 (CA), 259 (Staughton LJ), 270 (Butler-Sloss LJ). But cf *Lawrence David Ltd v Ashton* [1989] ICR 123 (CA), 135 (Balcombe LJ): the exception applies only if the injunction will completely or largely have run its course before trial.

[11] *Cambridge Nutrition Ltd v British Broadcasting Corp* [1990] 3 All ER 523 (CA), 535 (Kerr LJ).

[12] [1992] 1 AC 191, 226.

ADEQUACY OF DAMAGES

Damages are rarely an adequate remedy for a claimant in confidentiality cases. Where the claimant's interest is personal (ie, the claimant seeks to keep personal secrets secret), it seems self-evident that damages will be a poor substitute for specific enforcement of the defendant's obligations. So too where government secrets are involved.[13] But this is also often true even where the information is commercially confidential. For instance, where a person intends to use arguably confidential information to compete against the claimant, the difficulties of quantifying loss or profits militates against regarding damages as an adequate remedy.[14] So too if the defendant is unlikely to be able to pay damages if they are awarded.[15]

When *will* damages be an adequate remedy? There seem to be relatively few cases. In *Douglas v Hello! Ltd*,[16] the Court of Appeal held that two celebrities and the magazine to which they had sold the 'exclusive' story of their wedding would be adequately compensated in damages if a rival publication published unauthorised photographs arguably obtained in breach of confidence. The decision seems questionable as a matter of fact, given the difficulties of computing loss,[17] but it does at least indicate the sort of circumstances in which damages might be adequate. The dispute was seen as essentially and primarily commercial. The Douglases were not primarily concerned to suppress entirely the publication of private information, but rather concerned with who it was published by. And the damage likely to be suffered by them and the magazine to which they had sold the 'exclusive' right to cover their wedding was discrete: it related to two issues of a particular magazine, and sales and advertising revenue, rather than to an ongoing stream of profits in a competitive market where the very structure of the market might be changed by the defendant's activities.

Besides the adequacy of damages as compensation for the claimant if an injunction is refused, one has also to consider the adequacy of damages for the defendant if it is wrongly granted. A cross-undertaking in damages will be required. But will it be of any value? The direct loss of earnings by an employee who is temporarily prevented from working is easy enough to quantify.[18] There is more difficulty, however, in assessing long-term or remoter damage, for instance to the employee's career prospects by being kept out of the market,[19] or

[13] As in *Attorney-General v Guardian Newspapers Ltd* [1987] 1 WLR 1248 (HL).

[14] *Sun Valley Foods Ltd v Vincent* [2000] FSR 825, 838 (Jonathan Parker J).

[15] *Lawrence David Ltd v Ashton* [1989] ICR 123, 134 (Balcombe LJ).

[16] [2001] QB 967.

[17] It is ironic that, an injunction having been refused on the basis that the Douglases' interests were commercial and compensable in damages, damages were then limited on the ground that the Douglases' interests were . . . not commercial! See *Douglas v Hello! Ltd (No 3)* [2005] EWCA Civ 595, [2006] QB 125, [243]–[249].

[18] *Lawrence-David Ltd v Ashton* [1989] ICR 123, 134 (Balcombe LJ).

[19] *Ibid*; *Sun Valley Foods Ltd v Vincent* [2000] FSR 825, 839 (Jonathan Parker J).

damage to the competitive position of a trading company. The possibility that irreparable loss will be suffered if a financially precarious defendant is forced into insolvency by the injunction, while not decisive, should be considered.[20] So too, of course, must any risk that the claimant will be unable to meet any order made on the cross-undertaking in damages, although in an appropriate case an injunction could be granted even though an impecunious claimant was unlikely to be able to do so.[21]

OTHER FACTORS

Having taken into account the merits of the claim (to the extent that it is proper to do so, as it frequently will be in confidentiality cases), and the degree to which the prejudice suffered by either side will be compensable (frequently limited), the court can consider any other factors relevant to the question whether it is just and convenient that an interlocutory injunction should be granted, including (for example) any prejudice likely to be suffered by third parties. The cases stress the importance of treating the *American Cyanamid* principles as guidelines, not as strict rules, retaining the necessary flexibility to grant or withhold interim injunctions as justice and convenience require.[22]

EFFECT ON THIRD PARTIES

Except in the case of injunctions *contra mundum*,[23] an interim injunction binds, as such, only those who are parties to the litigation.[24] Even where the injunction is expressed to prohibit the defendant from doing something 'by his employees or agents', the reference is:

> nothing other than a warning against wrongdoing to those persons who may by reason of their situation be thought easily to fall into the error of implicating themselves in a breach of the injunction by the defendant.[25]

The only person 'bound' by the order is the defendant.

[20] *Potters-Ballotini Ltd v Weston-Baker* [1977] RPC 202 (CA). The comments of May LJ in *Roger Bullivant Ltd v Ellis* [1987] ICR 464, 482, to the effect that it is *nihil ad rem* if an injunction drives the defendant into insolvency are dangerous. It is *nihil ad rem* if the injunction is properly granted; but it may (it is suggested) be very material to the question whether the injunction should be granted.

[21] *Bunn v BBC* [1999] FSR 70, 77 (Lightman J).

[22] *Hubbard v Vosper* [1972] 2 QB 84, 96 (Lord Denning MR); *Cambridge Nutrition Ltd v British Broadcasting Corp* [1990] 3 All ER 523, 535 (Kerr LJ).

[23] See pp 114–15, 120–21 above; such injunctions may be made on an interim basis.

[24] *Iveson v Harris* (1802) 7 Ves Jun 251; *Attorney-General v Times Newspapers Ltd* [1992] 1 AC 181, 203 (Lord Brandon).

[25] *Marengo v Daily Sketch and Sunday Graphic Ltd* [1948] 1 All ER 406 (HL), 407 (Lord Uthwatt).

Nevertheless, it is a contempt of court intentionally to interfere with or impede the due administration of justice. If a court, in order to preserve the secrecy of allegedly confidential information pending trial, orders that a party must not use or disclose it, and a third party—knowing of that order—discloses it, that third party may commit a contempt of court.[26] This is not because the third party has breached the order (he has not). It is rather because he has deliberately done something to thwart a state of affairs that, to his knowledge, the court has regarded as necessary in the interests of justice. The practical effect, however, is strikingly similar. So long as a person has notice that a court has decided to protect information by interim injunction pending trial, its deliberate disclosure is likely in most cases to be a contempt of court.

[26] *Attorney-General v Times Newspapers Ltd* [1992] 1 AC 191 (HL).

§ 23

Financial Remedies

A claimant who proves breach of confidence will normally be entitled to claim either damages as compensation for his loss, or an account of profits to disgorge the defendant's gain, but must elect between those remedies.

AS A MATTER OF history, the availability of different financial remedies for breach of confidence was bedevilled by entirely arbitrary distinctions[1] between the legal and equitable remedies. If confidentiality rested on an express or implied contract, enforceable at law, there was no difficulty in awarding compensatory damages; but it was open to question whether the claimant should be entitled to the restitutionary remedy of an account of profits.[2] Conversely, if the duty of confidence was equitable, there was no difficulty with an account of profits; but potential difficulty with the grant of damages, since if the disclosure had already occurred it seemed unlikely that damages could be awarded 'in lieu of an injunction' under Lord Cairns' Act.[3]

These teasing problems have stimulated academic discussion.[4] But whatever the juristic basis for the current position, it seems at least clear. First, damages are available for breach of confidence (whether or not it is also a breach of contract), either on the basis of a 'beneficent interpretation of Lord Cairns' Act'[5] or on an independent basis as a form of equitable compensation.[6] Secondly, whether or not the breach involves a breach of contract, an account of profits may be ordered for breach of confidence.[7]

[1] '[N]othing short of sophistry': *Attorney-General v Blake* [2001] 1 AC 268 (HL), 285 (Lord Nicholls).

[2] See *Attorney-General v Blake*, *ibid*, which removed the problem.

[3] Now s 50 of the Supreme Court Act 1981. See *Robb v Green* [1895] 2 QB 315 (CA), *Malone v Metropolitan Police Commissioner* [1979] Ch 344, 360 (Megarry V-C).

[4] See Toulson & Phipps, paras 2–067 to 2–089; Gurry, pp 428–42; J Beatson, 'Damages for Breach of Confidence' (1991) 107 *LQR* 209.

[5] *Attorney-General v Guardian Newspapers Ltd* (*No 2*) [1990] 1 AC 109, 286 (Lord Goff).

[6] Toulson & Phipps, para 2–083.

[7] *Attorney-General v Guardian Newspapers Ltd* (*No 2*) [1990] 1 AC 109 (HL); *Attorney-General v Blake* [2001] 1 AC 268 (HL).

AVAILABILITY OF THE ACCOUNT

Where commercially valuable confidential information is misused, an account is available 'almost as a matter of course'.[8] In principle, however, it remains an equitable remedy which is granted or withheld as a matter of discretion. The most likely practical situations in which an account might be refused are (*a*) if the claimant's behaviour makes it unjust to order an account, in particular if there has been unreasonable delay taking action or acquiescence in the defendant's acts, or (*b*) where disproportionate hardship would be caused to a morally innocent defendant if he was obliged to account, in particular because he has changed his position in good faith.[9] But the discretion cannot be rigidly restricted. It is possible that an account might be refused if there are other 'compelling circumstances' to do so. For instance, if the defendant would probably have been licensed by the claimant to use the information in any event, the court might consider that the award of damages measured by the value of the licence to be an entirely adequate remedy,[10] and an account of profits to involve the risk that the claimant would be unfairly enriched. Conceivably, too, the court might refuse to order an account if the practical difficulties of taking it were so profound as to be unmanageable.

ELECTION

A claimant may not have *both* an account of profits *and* damages.[11] If both remedies are available, she has a 'choice' and must elect which to have.[12] The election generally is to be made at the time of judgment. But the court may decide liability first, and then grant a declaration that the claimant is entitled to elect, thereafter permitting the claimaint a reasonable opportunity to consider which remedy to choose.[13] Either remedy, however, may be freely combined with an injunction.

[8] *Attorney-General v Blake* [2001] 1 AC 268 (HL), 287 (Lord Nicholls).

[9] See § 19 above. An account was refused in *Satnam Investments Ltd v Dunlop Heywood & Co Ltd* [1999] 3 All ER 652 (CA), 672, on grounds that it would be disproportionate.

[10] By analogy to *Fyffes Group Ltd v Templeman* [2000] 2 Lloyd's Rep 643, 672 (Toulson J).

[11] *Sed quaere* if the damages claimed are *exemplary*. There is an inconsistency between claiming a restitution and compensation. But there does not seem to be any inherent contradiction between restitution and punishment.

[12] *Attorney-General v Blake* [2001] 1 AC 268 (HL), 286 (Lord Nicholls). See also *Caxton Publishing Co Ltd v Sutherland Publishing Co Ltd* [1939] AC 178 (HL) (copyright); *Peter Pan Manufacturing Corp v Corsets Silhouette Ltd* [1964] 1 WLR 96.

[13] *Island Records Ltd v Tring International plc* [1996] 1 WLR 1256.

§ 24

Assessment of Damages

(1) Where damages are assessed, the claimant is entitled to recover the financial loss foreseeably caused by the breach of confidence, including any loss of profit. If information is commercially valuable, that loss may be assessed at the fair value of the information.

(2) In cases involving the misuse of personal information, a sum may also be awarded to compensate the claimant for distress caused by the misuse.

(3) In an appropriate case, exemplary damages might be awarded for breach of confidence.

FINANCIAL LOSS

THE OBJECT OF an award of damages for breach of confidence is the same as the object of such an award in tort generally: to put the injured party in the position he would have been in if the wrong had not been committed.[1] The position is the same if the duty of confidence is contractual. For there the conventional question ('What would be the claimant's position if the contract had been honoured?') leads in practice to the same place. In either case, the claimant obtains damages (including damages for loss of profit) which compensate not merely for out-of-pocket or 'reliance' losses, but for 'expectation' losses too. That is hardly surprising, since the very object of the action for breach of confidence is to vindicate the claimant's 'reasonable expectation'.

There are, however, various ways in which that objective may be pursued. It may be done by carrying out a detailed inquiry into the position the claimant would have been in if the confidence had been respected, thereby arriving at an assessment of the actual loss suffered (including loss of profits).[2] The claimant

[1] *Dowson Mason Ltd v Potter* [1986] 1 WLR 1419 (CA), 1422 (Sir Edward Eveleigh), relying on *General Tire & Rubber Co v Firestone Tyre & Rubber Co Ltd* [1975] 1 WLR 819 (HL), 824 (Lord Wilberforce) (a patent case); *Indata Equipment Supplies Ltd v ACL Ltd* [1998] 1 BCLC 412 (CA), 425 (Otton LJ). See also *Cadbury Schweppes Inc v FBI Foods Ltd* [2000] FSR 491 (Sup Ct Can).

[2] This was the approach taken in *Dowson Mason Ltd v Potter* [1986] 1 WLR 1419 (CA) and *Douglas v Hello! Ltd (No 7)* [2004] EMLR 11, in which the judgment on damages was affirmed by the House of Lords, [2007] UKHL 21, [2007] 2 WLR 920. It was also the approach taken in *Universal Thermosensors Ltd v Hibben* [1992] 1 WLR 840, albeit that no substantial loss was found to have been caused.

is entitled to recover not only for the actual misuse of confidential information by the defendant, but for all loss foreseeably caused by that misuse including subsequent republication by third parties.[3]

In practice, such an ad hoc inquiry into the loss suffered may be difficult. An alternative approach is to attempt to 'value the information', by asking in effect what the claimant would have charged to licence its use. Where the breach has diminished the value of confidential information, the amount of that reduction in value may be taken as the measure of loss.[4] That approach was taken in *Seager v Copydex Ltd (No 2)*.[5] Its limits, however, should be carefully noted. The object of such an exercise always remains to put a figure on the amount of loss actually suffered. It is not therefore an appropriate measure to adopt where it is clear that the claimant would not have exploited the information commercially at all.[6] Nor, it is suggested, could resort to a notional licence fee be used as a way of obtaining substantial damages in a case[7] where a detailed consideration of the evidence showed that no loss had in fact been caused by any misuse of confidential information.

Where damages are assessed based on the value of the information if it were traded, the result is similar to what would have been achieved if the claimant had been awarded a *quantum meruit*, that is a remedy to prevent the defendant from being unjustly enriched by obtaining information without paying for it.[8] But the view taken in the cases seems to be that this is a coincidence. The valuation is for the purposes of awarding damages (ie compensation for the claimant's loss), not restitution (reversal of the defendant's gain). In most cases this really makes no difference: the claimant's loss (of the ability to charge the defendant to use information) is the same as the defendant's gain (using the information without paying for it), so that 'reversing' the loss and 'reversing' the enrichment amount to the same thing. To argue about whether the damages are restitutionary or compensatory is often to argue about whether the glass is half full or half empty. But it can matter; and where it does matter, the position seems to be that the compensation rationale is applied. Were the aim restitutionary, it would not be inappropriate to refuse to award such a sum based on the claimant's lack of desire voluntarily to commercialise the information.[9] The

[3] As happened in *Douglas v Hello Ltd (No 7)* [2004] EMLR 11. The case assumes that the test of remoteness is foreseeability: but-for causation in itself is not enough: *Douglas v Hello! Ltd (No 3)* [2005] EWCA Civ 595, [2006] QB 125, [240].

[4] As in *Talbot v General Television Corp Pty* [1981] RPC 1 (Sup Ct Vict).

[5] [1969] 1 WLR 809 (CA).

[6] *Douglas v Hello! Ltd (No 3)* [2005] EWCA Civ 595, [2006] QB 125, [243]–[249].

[7] Such as *Universal Thermosensors Ltd v Hibben* [1992] 1 WLR 840.

[8] See G Jones, 'Restitution of Benefits Obtained in Breach of Another's Confidence' (1970) 86 *LQR* 463; Goff and G Jones, *The Law of Restitution*, 7th edn (London, 2006), para 34–022; G Virgo, *Principles of the Law of Restitution*, 2nd edn (Oxford, 2006), 529.

[9] As in *Douglas v Hello! Ltd (No 3)*, [2005] EWCA Civ 595, [2006] QB 125, [243]–[249], which is criticised for this very reason in Goff and G Jones, *The Law of Restitution*, 7th edn (London, 2006), para 34–023, for precisely this reason.

appropriate restitutionary remedy in breach of confidence cases appears to be an account of profits, and not a *quantum meruit*.

NON-FINANCIAL LOSS

In cases involving the misuse of personal information, damages for injury to feeling may be awarded. The cases suggest that awards under this head are generally small, a matter of a few thousand pounds.[10] (Though much, of course, would depend on the nature of the information.) Aggravated damages can be awarded.[11]

EXEMPLARY DAMAGES

If the basic requirements laid down in *Rookes v Barnard*[12] are satisfied (and in particular where the defendant cynically calculated that its profits from wrongdoing would exceed any damages payable), there seems no reason in principle why exemplary damages should not be awarded for breach of confidence.[13] Since the power to award such damages is no longer regarded as confined by narrow considerations of the particular cause of action relied upon,[14] it would be arbitrary to refuse to countenance any award in a breach of confidence case.[15]

The function of exemplary damages is to ensure that the law adequately deters wrongdoing, where even full compensation for the claimant's loss might not achieve that end. Where the profits actually made by the defendant exceed the claimant's loss, the account of profits can prevent unjust enrichment, and goes some way towards ensuring that cynical wrongdoing is not encouraged.[16] That may not be a complete solution, however, since it fails to deal with cases

[10] *McKennitt v Ash* [2005] EWHC 3003, [2006] EMLR 178 (£5,000); *Douglas v Hello! Ltd (No 3)* [2005] EWCA Civ 595, [2006] QB 125 (£3,750); *Archer v Williams* [2003] EMLR 869 (£2,500); *Cornelius v de Taranto* [2001] EMLR 12 (£3,000); *Campbell v MGN Ltd* [2002] EMLR 30 (£2,500: aggravated damages of £1,000 in addition). The award of £1,000 in *Williams v Settle* [1960] 1 WLR 1072 seems high by modern standards, admittedly in a serious case.

[11] *Campbell v MGN Ltd* [2004] UKHL 22, [2004] 2 AC 457, [35] (Lord Nicholls). The judge's award, upheld by the House of Lords, included aggravated damages.

[12] [1964] AC 1129 (HL), 1226–7 (Lord Devlin).

[13] There is authority in New Zealand that they might be: *Aquaculture Corp v New Zealand Green Mussel Co Ltd* [1990] 3 NZLR 299, 301. In *Douglas v Hello! Ltd (No 3)* [2003] EWHC 786, [2003] 3 All ER 996, Lindsay J assumed that they might be awarded, but made no award. See also A Burrows, 'Remedial Coherence and Punitive Damages in Equity' in S Degeling and J Edelman (eds), *Equity in Commercial Law* (Pyrmont, 2005), ch 15.

[14] *Kuddus v Chief Constable of Leicestershire Constabulary* [2001] UKHL 29, [2002] 2 AC 122.

[15] A contrary view has been taken in New South Wales: *Harris v Digital Pulse Pty Ltd* [2003] NSWC 10, 56 NSWLR 298.

[16] As is pointed out in Goulding et al, *Employee Competition: Covenants, Confidentiality and Garden Leave* (Oxford, 2007), para 3.150.

where the cynical *calculation* can be shown to have occurred, but proof of the profits is impossible or excessively difficult. The position seems to be that such damages are theoretically available, but unlikely to be of practical importance in the vast run of cases.

§ 25

Assessment of Profits

(1) Where an account of profits is taken, the object of the inquiry is to ascertain the profit made by the defendant from the misuse of protected information.
(2) The profit is normally assessed by taking the entire revenue derived by the defendant from products embodying the protected information and deducting the costs of manufacturing and an appropriate allowance for overheads and expenditure. In some cases it may be appropriate to apportion the award in order to make allowance for profits earned legitimately.
(3) In an appropriate case, the court may be willing to allow an additional allowance for the defendant's time and skill.

THE OBJECT OF AN ACCOUNT

THE OBJECT OF an account of profits was lucidly explained by the High Court of Australia in *Dart Industries Inc v Decor Corp Pty Ltd*:

> The equitable principle of an account of profits is not to compensate the [claimant], nor to fix a fair price for the infringing product, but to prevent the unjust enrichment of the defendant.[1]

To that end, in the picturesque language of the mid-nineteenth century, the court:

> takes from the wrongdoer all the profits he has made by his piracy, and gives them to the party who has been wronged.[2]

The essential aim and difficulty of an account is to identify what profits have been 'made by the piracy', or 'what profits have been caused, in a legal sense, by [the wrongful] acts'.[3]

[1] [1994] FSR 567, 575. See also *Potton v Yorkclose Ltd* [1990] FSR 11, 16 (Millett J).
[2] *Colburn v Simms* (1843) 2 Hare 543, 560 (Wigram V-C).
[3] *Celanese International Corp v BP Chemicals Ltd* [1999] RPC 203, 219 (Laddie J).

THE METHOD ADOPTED

The starting point appears from *Peter Pan Manufacturing Corp v Corsets Silhouette Ltd*.[4] There the defendants had misused confidential information in the course of manufacturing bras. The defendants argued that they ought not to be obliged to account for all their profit from the sale of the infringing bras. They could, they said, have earned at least part of their profit from the sale of similar bras that would not have infringed: only the 'excess profits' should be accounted for. Pennycuick J rejected that argument, holding that the account was to be taken applying some simple principles: (*a*) What has the defendant expended in manufacturing the goods? (*b*) What is the price that has been received? 'And the difference is profit'.[5]

In principle that is correct, and is consistent with the approach taken in other cases (for instance trade mark cases). If the defendant has *in fact* used confidential information to make profit, it is no answer that he *could* have made a similar profit without the use of such information. The money earned by selling the bras that the defendants in *Peter Pan* had sold was *in fact* made using confidential information. That similar profits might have been earned in some other, legitimate, way is irrelevant. As Laddie J pointed out in *Celanese International Corp v BP Chemicals Ltd*,[6] however, the converse also applies: the claimant takes the defendant as he finds him, and cannot complain that the defendant ought to have made greater profits than were actually made.

Nevertheless, there are cases in which such an approach is not fair, for just as in patent cases it is 'unreasonable to give the [claimant] profits which were not earned by the use of his invention',[7] so in a breach of confidence case it would be unreasonable to give the claimant profits which were not earned by the misuse of his information. Suppose, for example, that a magazine includes a single article containing confidential information. Is it right that the defendant should pay to the claimant *all* the profit earned by the sale of that issue of the magazine? That seems an extravagant proposition. In such a case, the defendant not only *might* have made much of its profit without infringing, but it can truly be said that it *would* have made much of its profit without infringing. As in a copyright case, one would expect apportionment to reflect the contribution the breach of confidence actually made to the magazine as a whole. So, too, if it is clear that the defendants would have manufactured the same product, but at greater cost if they had not made use of some cost-saving confidential information. There, as in *Sidell v Vickers*[8] some apportionment is necessary—there has to be

[4] [1964] 1 WLR 96.

[5] *Ibid*, 108.

[6] [1999] RPC 203, 221.

[7] *United Horse-Shoe and Nail Co Ltd v John Stewart & Co* (1888) 13 App Cas 401 (HL), 412 (Lord Watson).

[8] (1892) 9 RPC 152 (CA).

a comparison of the profit that *would* have been earned innocently with that which was in fact earned illicitly, and the defendant accounts for the difference. (In other cases, different methods of apportionment may be appropriate. The calculation can be difficult, but the approach required is one of broad fairness, not arithmetic exactness.[9])

Properly understood, it is suggested, there is no inconsistency between these cases. It is simply a question of taking a realistic view of the facts on the ground in answering the basic question: 'What profit did the defendant earn by the misuse?' In *Peter Pan*, every penny made by the defendant from selling the bras was made from the misuse of the claimant's information—and it was no answer to say that a similar sum might have been made in some other way. In other cases, such as the example given above of the magazine, it is unrealistic to say that every penny from the sale of the magazine is made as a result of the misuse of the claimant's information, and necessary to arrive at some apportionment.

There are also cases where the account may need to extend beyond the actual infringing acts. Suppose, for example, that a defendant publishes a book, B_1, revealing confidential information. Once that book is published, confidentiality is lost.[10] The defendant then *re*publishes the same information in a second book B_2. The publication of B_2 is not itself a breach of confidence; it could not, for instance, be enjoined.[11] But it is surely arguable that the profits made on B_2 are as much due to the misuse of confidential information as those made from B_1, since it is the publication of B_1 which clears the way (by destroying confidentiality) for B_2. In such a case it is suggested, no special principle is needed to make the defendant accountable for the profits from B_2: they are recoverable because, causally, they all flow from the misuse of protected information.[12]

ALLOWANCES

The account of profits is restitutionary, not punitive. As is evident from *Peter Pan*,[13] any account of profits necessarily involves making allowance for the cost of manufacturing or producing the articles from which the profit is made: it is an account of *profits*, not of *revenue*.[14] Beyond that, the defendant will also

[9] *My Kinda Town Ltd v Soll* [1983] RPC 15, 58 (Slade J); *Potton v Yorkclose Ltd* [1990] FSR 11, 19 (Millett J).

[10] See § 7.

[11] Subject, perhaps, to an argument for an injunction to prevent a person profiting from his past wrong.

[12] This appears to have been the view of Lord Goff: *Attorney-General v Guardian Newspapers Ltd* (*No 2*) [1990] 1 AC 109, 288.

[13] [1964] 1 WLR 96.

[14] But perhaps no allowance for the cost of wrongfully acquiring the confidential information: *Attorney-General v Guardian Newspapers Ltd* (*No 2*) [1990] 1 AC 109 (HL), 262 (Lord Keith). Lord Keith's explanation, however, is hard to understand, and failure to deduct could result in double-accounting. Lord Donaldson MR saw 'no escape' from the conclusion that the costs of obtaining the information were deductible: [1990] 1 AC 109, 198.

generally be permitted an allowance for a proportion of its general overheads that contributed to earning the profit.[15]

It is possible, in an appropriate case, that an accounting person may be held entitled to a further allowance, reflecting the positive contribution in time and skill that he has made to earning the profits.[16] It seems inconceivable that any such allowance would be allowed in favour of a conscious wrongdoer. But where the breach of confidence is innocent, it might be thought preferable to the outright refusal to allow any account.

[15] See *Dart Industries Inc v Decor Corp Pty Ltd* [1994] FSR 567 (HC Australia), where the question is extensively discussed.

[16] *Boardman v Phipps* [1967] 2 AC 46 (HL), and the principles set out by Wilberforce J at first instance in *Boardman,* [1964] 1 WLR 993, 1018; applied by Robert Goff J in *Redwood Music Ltd v Chappell* [1982] RPC 109. But the allowance is not in principle an allowance of profit: *Potton v Yorkclose Ltd* [1990] FSR 11, 18 (Millett J). In *Guinness plc v Saunders* [1990] 2 AC 663, 694, Lord Templeman suggested such an allowance would only be made in 'exceptional circumstances'.

§ 26

Limitation

(1) A claim for damages or equitable compensation for breach of confidence—

(a) must, if founded on a contractual duty of confidence, be brought within six years after the breach took place;

(b) must, if founded on an equitable duty of confidence, be brought within six years after the breach took place, and may in an appropriate case be regarded as time barred earlier (*i*) if there is acquiescence by the claimant after the breach or (*ii*) (possibly) if the claim relates to the misuse of false information, one year after the breach took place.

(2) A claim for an account of profits for breach of confidence—

(a) must, if founded on a contractual duty of confidence, be brought within six years after the breach took place, and may in an appropriate case be regarded as time barred earlier if there is acquiescence by the claimant after the breach;

(b) must, if founded on an equitable duty of confidence, be brought within the same period as a claim for damages (as set out in § 26 (1) (b)).

(3) A claim for an injunction to restrain a breach of confidence may be brought at any time, but may be refused if the claimant's delay in seeking relief amounts to laches or acquiescence.

(4) In this section—

'Acquiescence' occurs where the claimant's delay in seeking relief has, in all the circumstances, given rise to an impression that the claimant would not seek relief, and it would be unjust under the circumstances to grant relief.

'Laches' occurs where the claimant's delay in seeking relief makes it unjust in all the circumstances to grant relief.

IDENTIFYING THE RULES that govern the limitation of actions for breach of confidence is not straightforward. They depend on a rather complicated interaction between different parts of the Limitation Act 1980 and equitable principles. Because of the way the Limitation Act is drafted, the action for breach of confidence risks disappearing through the cracks. Not surprisingly, given the sort of conduct usually complained of, there appear to be very few reported cases on the statutory limitation of actions for breach of confidence. To some degree, therefore, the principles are a matter of speculation.

THE PATCHWORK OF RULES

There are two distinct bodies of rules: the statutory rules of the Limitation Act 1980 which prevent actions being brought more than a certain period after the cause of action accrued (limitation in the strict sense), and equitable principles of laches, acquiescence and application of statutory limitation 'by analogy'. Teasing out the rules applicable to breach of confidence involves working out which sets of rules apply and how they interact, and what they do.

Statutory limitation. The simplest is statutory limitation, which has three operating principles. The first is a matter of categorisation. The Limitation Act specifies rules applicable to different types of action. Three matter for present purposes: an action 'founded on a tort',[1] an action 'founded on a simple contract',[2] and an action 'for libel or slander . . . or other malicious falsehood'.[3] The categories identify the relevant limitation period. There is no rule that every claim known to the law must fall under some specified category. The second principle specifies the point at which time begins to run. So far as the present topic is concerned, that is in each case the date on which the 'cause of action accrued':[4] the earliest moment when every one of the facts necessary for a viable claim exists.[5] For our purposes that means the date on which information which is subject to a duty of confidence is misused (whether or not the claimant knows of that misuse, and whether or not the claimant suffers any harm by it). The third principle specifies a period of time, and provides that no action can be 'brought' (ie no court proceedings started[6]) after the expiry of that period. The leading characteristics of the Act are, therefore, rigidity and precision. It establishes a series of bright-lines: a bright-line category of claims, a bright-line point at which the claim accrues and limitation starts to run, and a bright line moment at which the axe falls. In some areas those bright lines are blurred by elements of statutory discretion, but none is relevant to the type of claim with which we are concerned.

The common law did not (apart from statute) impose any time limits on bringing claims. Equity, however, does and did, via three principles: laches, acquiescence, and the application of the common law limitation periods by analogy.

[1] Limitation Act 1980, s 2.
[2] *Ibid*, s 5.
[3] *Ibid*, s 4A
[4] This is the language used in ss 2, 4A and 5.
[5] *Coburn v Colledge* [1897] 1 QB 702 (CA).
[6] The key date is the date on which the claim form is issued by the court.

Laches and acquiescence. It is convenient to begin with acquiescence. The term, in equity, has two distinct meanings. It applies, first, to a case where a person stands by and permits an act to be done which causes him injury—acquiescence at the time of the conduct complained of. Such a person may be taken, albeit by inaction, to have consented to the act in question, and cannot be permitted to complain of it.[7] Used in that sense, 'aquiescence' has nothing to do with limitation or laches: it is an aspect of the rules dealing with consent.[8] 'Aquiescence' is used, secondly, to refer to a person who—after the conduct complained of has occurred—takes no active steps to complain of or obtain a remedy for it. If that apathy leads the wrongdoer to believe that the right in question has been abandoned, or induces the wrongdoer or a third party to incur a detriment which makes it unfair to permit the claimant to change her stance, equity may refuse to grant relief.[9]

Laches is a similar doctrine: so similar that it is hard to distinguish from acquiescence.[10] Its underlying principle is that there may come a point where the claimant's inaction makes it unfair to grant a remedy. It asks of the claimant whether there has been unreasonable delay in taking action. It asks of the defendant whether that delay is such that it either gives the objective impression that the claimant meant to give up any potential claim, or that it has caused such prejudice to the defendant or a third party that it would be unfair—inequitable—to grant relief. In breach of confidence cases it is this second sort of situation that is most likely to be important.

In *Nelson v Rye*[11] Laddie J pointed out that it can be 'misleading to approach the equitable defences of laches and acquiescence as if they consisted of a series of precisely defined hurdles over which a litigant must struggle before the defence is made out'.[12] The essential question is 'whether the balance of justice or injustice is in favour of granting the remedy or withholding it'.[13] In this respect it stands in marked contrast to the statutory rules on limitation which are (with certain well-defined exceptions) applied rigidly and without regard to whether they achieve a fair or an unfair result.

The flexible standards applied, and the manner in which they are applied, was classically explained by Lord Selborne in *Lindsay Petroleum Co v Hurd*:

> Now the doctrine of laches in Court of Equity is not an arbitrary or technical doctrine. Where it would be practically unjust to give a remedy, either because a party has, by his conduct, done that which might fairly be regarded as equivalent to a waiver of it,

[7] See, eg, *Duke of Leeds v Earl of Amherst* (1846) 2 Ph 117, 123 (Lord Cottenham); Meagher, Gummow and Lehane, para 36–005.

[8] See § 10. *Sunderland v Barclays Bank Ltd* (1938) 5 *Legal Decisions Affecting Bankers* 163, discussed p 51 above, is close to this.

[9] Meagher, Gummow & Lehane, para 36–094.

[10] To the extent that distinction may be necessary, a possible approach is suggested at p 144 below. In effect, it is suggested, 'acquiescence' is a particular sort of laches.

[11] [1996] 1 WLR 1368.

[12] *Ibid*, 1392.

[13] *Erlanger v New Sombrero Phosphate Co* (1878) 3 App Cas 1218 (HL), 1279 (Lord Blackburn).

> or where by his conduct and neglect he has, though perhaps not waiving that remedy, yet put the other party in a situation in which it would not be reasonable to place him if the remedy were afterwards to be asserted, in either of these cases, lapse of time and delay are most material. But in every case, if an argument against relief, which otherwise would be just, is founded upon mere delay, . . . the validity of that defence must be tried upon principles substantially equitable.[14]

Modern cases lay particular emphasis on the proposition that the defences are not 'arbitrary . . . or technical'—to the point, arguably, that they threaten to become unpredictably flexible. In *Frawley v Neill*[15] Aldous LJ rejected the application of any 'preconceived formula'. He stated that what was required was a 'broad approach, directed to ascertaining whether it would in all the circumstances be unconscionable for a party to be permitted to assert his beneficial right'.

The key factors to be considered are (*a*) how quickly one would reasonably have expected the claimant to act, (*b*) the extent of the delay, (*c*) the reasons for the delay, (*d*) how far the delay would reasonably have given the defendant a positive impression that the claimant intended to take no action, (*e*) how far the defendant has suffered any prejudice as a result of the delay. There remains an unresolved debate whether *mere* delay can amount to laches.[16] The better view is probably that it cannot; but in practice there is never much difficulty in extreme cases in finding that the delay has lasted so long as to amount to waiver of the remedy,[17] or identifying some prejudice (such as failing recollections or possible loss of evidence) which converts 'mere' delay into something worse.

Application of the Limitation Act by analogy. Another technique to which equity may have recourse where no statutory limitation period properly applies is the application of the Limitation Act 'by analogy'. Even if an equitable claim does not strictly fall within one of the statutory categories, equitable relief may still be refused if the claim bears a sufficiently close resemblance to a category of claim that does. So, for instance, in *Cia de Seguros Imperio v Heath (REBX) Ltd*[18] the Court of Appeal held that an action for breach of statutory duty does not fall into any statutory category—but that the six-year period applicable to claims in tort should be applied by analogy.

[14] (1874) LR 5 PC 221, 239–40. In *Erlanger, ibid*, 1279, Lord Blackburn said that this gave a 'more distinct and definite rule' than any other decided case. It has, as Meagher, Gummow & Lehane point out (para 36–025), been applied 'time without number': see, eg, *Nelson v Rye* [1996] 1 WLR 1368, or *Nwakobi v Nzekwu* [1964] 1 WLR 1019 (PC).

[15] *The Times*, 5 Apr 1999. The quotations are taken from the transcript of the Court of Appeal judgments. The case has been approved by the Court of Appeal in *Patel v Shah* [2005] EWCA Civ 157 and *Re Loftus* [2006] EWCA Civ 1124, [2007] 1 WLR 591.

[16] See Meagher, Gummow & Lehane, paras 36–070 to 36–080.

[17] As, eg, in *Cluett Peabody & Co Inc v McIntyre Hogg Marsh & Co Ltd* [1958] RPC 335.

[18] [2001] 1 WLR 112 (CA)

THE INTERACTION OF THE PRINCIPLES

The way the principles interact depends on a combination of the claim made and the remedy sought.

Common law damages plus statutory limitation. Where common law damages are sought for a claim that is subject to a statutory limitation period, only the Limitation Act applies. If the claim is made out of time, it fails. If it is made in time, it proceeds—and there is no possibility of refusing relief on grounds of laches or acquiescence. It is from this principle that § 26 (1) (a) derives. If the cause of action is for a breach of a contractual duty of confidence, then the Limitation Act specifies a six-year limitation period from the date of breach.[19] And if the remedy sought is damages for breach of contract, then neither laches nor acquiescence has any part to play.

Account plus statutory limitation. Where an account is sought for a claim that is subject to a statutory limitation period the claim for an account must be brought within the statutory limitation period applicable to the claim generally.[20] But if the remedy sought is an account *in equity*, as in practice it always is, then it is possible that relief might be refused on grounds of 'acquiescence or otherwise' even if brought within the limitation period.[21] There are thus two separate sets of rules that might apply cumulatively: a fixed and rigid statutory period, and a flexible discretionary period which might be used to shorten (but not to lengthen) that fixed period.

There is one further complication. Where there is a statutory limitation period, there is respectable authority that the doctrine of laches does not apply—on the theory that if the statute 'permits' one X years to bring an action you must be 'entitled' to wait until the end of that period.[22] The logic of that approach is questionable. The Limitation Act prescribes times after which an action might not be brought. But it would not seem to follow as a matter of necessary implication that it confers a positive right to delay to the uttermost end of the period; indeed section 36 (2) which expressly preserves the power to refuse equitable relief on grounds of 'acquiescence or otherwise' suggests the contrary. But, whether flawed or not, the principle seems to be clearly established, and was accepted by the Court of Appeal in *Re Loftus*.[23] It must be taken to be the law.

It follows that, where a statutory period applies to the claim—as it does for a claim for a contractual breach of confidence—*laches* will not be deployed to refuse an account. But *acquiescence* is treated differently: it may still apply.[24] This

[19] Limitation Act 1980, s 5. This was the position in *Christofi v Barclays Bank plc* [2000] 1 WLR 937 (CA), a claim for damages for breach of a duty of confidence owed by a bank.

[20] Limitation Act 1980, s 23.

[21] *Ibid*, s 36 (2).

[22] *Archbold v Scully* (1861) 9 HLC 360 (HL), 383 (Lord Wensleydale); *Re Pauling* [1962] 1 WLR 86, 115 (Wilberforce J) affirmed [1964] Ch 303, 353 (CA).

[23] [2006] EWCA Civ 1124, [2007] 1 WLR 591, [35]–[37] (Chadwick LJ).

[24] *Re Loftus, ibid*, [35]–[36] (Chadwick LJ).

is regrettable, for it makes it necessary to distinguish between laches and acquiescence. Yet the authorities seem to treat them together, and almost as synonymous. The solution seems to be along these lines. Laches, pure and simple, applies where the claimant's delay makes it unfair for the defendant to be visited with the remedy sought, but does not go so far as to give the impression that the claimant has positively accepted the defendant's conduct. Acquiescence applies where the claimant's delay, on its own or in conjunction with other positive conduct, gives rise to the appearance that the claimant intends to take no action. It therefore more closely resembles a form of estoppel (conduct tantamount to a representation that rights have been given up[25]) or waiver ('that which might fairly be regarded as equivalent to a waiver'[26]) than does laches in its pure form.

It is from this principle, therefore, that one derives the rule stated in § 26 (2) (a). If the claim is founded on a contract, a statutory limitation period of six years applies to it.[27] The claim for an account is treated the same way.[28] Even within that time, however, the remedy (which is equitable) may be refused if the claimant's conduct has led the defendant to believe that no account would be claimed and to act on that belief (acquiescence)[29] but not if, although it might otherwise be thought unfair to grant relief, the defendant has not been led positively to believe that a remedy would not be pursued (laches).[30]

Claim for an injunction or other equitable relief plus statutory limitation. Here the position is different. Even where a statutory limitation period applies, the Limitation Act permits a claim to be made 'out of time' for equitable remedies, including injunctions.[31] To such claims *only* the equitable doctrines of laches and acquiescence apply, and both apply.[32] The rule in § 26 (3) derives from this principle.

Claim for equitable relief and no statutory limitation period. In such a case the equitable principles apply: relief may be refused on grounds of laches, or acquiescence, or by the application of the Limitation Act by analogy to a similar claim which does fall within a statutory category.

THE APPLICATION OF THE PRINCIPLES

The simple cases have already been dealt with: they are set out in § 26 (1) (a), § 26 (2) (a) and § 26 (3). They are not open to much argument or doubt. The

[25] *Nwakobi v Nzweku* [1964] 1 WLR 1019 (PC), 1024 (Viscount Radcliffe): 'that type of acquiescence which, when analysed, operates as an estoppel, because it has led the defendant to alter his position on the faith of the established inaction'.

[26] *Lindsay Petroleum Co v Hurd* (1874) LR 5 PC 221, 239 (Lord Selborne).

[27] Limitation Act 1980, s 5.

[28] *Ibid*, s 23.

[29] *Ibid*, s 36 (2) and *Re Loftus* [2006] EWCA Civ 1124, [2007] 1 WLR 591, [35]–[36].

[30] See the cases cited at n 22 above.

[31] Limitation Act 1980, s 36 (1).

[32] *Re Loftus* [2006] EWCA Civ 1124, [2007] 1 WLR 591, disapproving suggestions to the contrary in *Gwembe Valley Development Co Ltd v Koshy (No 3)* [2003] EWCA Civ 1048, [2004] BCLC 131.

interesting and difficult cases are those dealt with in § 26 (1) (b) and § 26 (2) (b)—that is claims for breach of a purely equitable duty of confidence, not 'founded on contract', where the remedy sought is damages or an account of profits. There are two sources of doubt. (*a*) Is a claim for breach of an equitable duty of confidence subject to any statutory limitation rule at all? (*b*) If it is subject to a statutory limitation rule, is the claim for damages for its breach a claim for 'equitable relief'?

There is really only one statutory category into which a claim for breach of an equitable duty of confidence might fall: the category of 'tort' to which section 2 of the Limitation Act 1980 applies a six year limitation period. The act contains no definition of 'tort'. There are two possible approaches. One approach would be to treat 'tort' as a compendious term applying to any form of civil wrong whose essence is that a breach of duty by the defendant has caused the claimant damage—a functional approach[33] On that basis, a claim for breach of confidence might well be regarded as a tort, even if it is an 'equitable' tort. There is no doubt that lawyers do talk about the 'tort' of breach of confidence.[34] On the other hand, if looked at from a historical point of view, torts can be seen as essentially and necessarily 'common law' creatures—using 'common law' in contradistinction to 'equity'. Breach of confidence is not a 'tort' in that sense.[35] On that basis, a claim for breach of an *equitable* duty is not capable of being a tort within the meaning of section 2.[36]

This dovetails with the second question. Is the claim for damages a claim for an equitable remedy, to which section 36 applies? A claim for equitable compensation is presumably a claim for an equitable remedy.[37] But what about damages under section 50 of the Supreme Court Act 1981, if this is how the grant

[33] As appears to have been adopted in *R v Secretary of State for Transport, ex parte Factortame Ltd* (*No* 7) [2001] 1 WLR 942, [149]–[150] (Judge Toulmin QC).

[34] For instance, there is a section on breach of confidence in textbooks on tort: K Oliphant (ed), *The Law of Tort*, 2nd edn (London, Butterworths, 2007), ch 24; AM Dugdale and MA Jones (eds), *Clerk & Lindsell on Torts,* 19th edn (London, 2006) ch 28. See also judicial references to the 'tort' of breach of confidence in, eg *Venables v News Group Newspapers Ltd* [2001] Fam 430, 448 (Butler-Sloss P); *Campbell v MGN Ltd* [2002] EWCA Civ 1373, [2003] QB 633, [69]; *McKennitt* v *Ash* [2006] EWCA Civ 1714, [2007] 3 WLR 194, [8]; and *Lord Browne of Madingley v Associated Newspapers Ltd* [2007] EWCA Civ 295, [2007] 3 WLR 289, [22]. That list is not comprehensive. The description of breach of confidence as a 'tort' seems to be regarded as perfectly natural.

[35] See *Kitechnology BV v Unicor GmbH Plastmaschinen* [1995] FSR 765, 777 (Evans LJ) in which it was held that a claim for breach of confidence is not a 'tort' for the purposes of (what is now) Art 5 (3) of Reg 44/2001/EC. Evans LJ referred to *Metall und Rohstoff AG v Donaldson Lufkin & Jenrette Inc* [1990] 1 QB 391, 474, where the Court of Appeal approved the statement that 'No civil injury is to be classed as a tort if it is only a breach of trust or some other merely equitable obligation. The reason for this exclusion is historical only. The law of torts is in its origin a part of the common law, as distinguished from equity, and it was unknown to the Court of Chancery'.

[36] *R v Secretary of State for Transport, ex parte Factortame* (*No* 7) [2001] 1 WLR 942, [150], exemplifies the ambiguity. In defining 'tort' broadly, Judge Toulmin referred to breach of a non-contractual duty which gives a private law right to recover damages 'at common law'. Does 'common law' add or mean anything, since Judge Toulmin clearly intended to include statutory torts (which are not 'common law' in one sense of the word) and EC torts (which are not 'common law' in any sense of the word)? Does it connote a distinction with damages in equity?

[37] *Cia de Seguros Imperio v Heath (REBX) Ltd* [2001] 1 WLR 112, 119 (Waller LJ).

of damages for breach of confidence is to be explained? This is a single section, which deals comprehensively with the power to award damages. It is by no means obvious why, more than a century after the institutional merger of the courts of equity and common law, the same remedy granted under the same statutory power should be regarded sometimes as an 'equitable remedy' and sometimes as a 'common law remedy'. Yet there is authority that it is.[38]

There is no easy answer to these questions; probably they can be largely avoided in practice for reasons which will become apparent. But it is suggested that the better answer, if one is needed, is that the claim for damages for breach of an equitable duty of confidence is to be treated, through-and-through, as an equitable claim for equitable relief, and not as a tort claim for damages. It follows that no statutory limitation period as such applies to it. This appears to have been the conclusion reached by the Court of Appeal in *Dutton v Spink & Beeching (Sales) Ltd*.[39]

It is likely, even so, that equity will apply a common law limitation period by analogy. In general, the relevant analogy will be to the tort claim, giving a period of six years.[40] Since this is no different from the period which would be applied if the claim were tortious in the strict sense of that word, it ought to be unnecessary to resolve that issue. It follows, second, that the doctrine of acquiescence at least will be applied to such claims as well; it is possible that laches may also apply, but are unlikely to matter. It is from these principles that § 26 (1) (b) and § 26 (2) (b) derive.

There is, however, one interesting possibility if the equitable wrong of breach of confidence is not regarded as a tort within the meaning of section 2 of the Limitation Act. Since the limitation period is applied only 'by analogy' there is some flexibility as to how the analogy is drawn. One potentially attractive aspect of this approach would be that it could allow the court to apply a period by analogy to the one-year limitation period for defamation and malicious falsehood[41] in cases where the information in question was alleged to be false. That might be desirable, since it could lay to rest the concern that claimants might frame their claim as a claim for breach of confidence precisely in order to avoid those limitation periods.

[38] *Joyce v Joyce* [1978] 1 WLR 1170, 1173 (Megarry V-C).

[39] [1977] 1 All ER 287, 293 (Goff LJ).

[40] See, for similar conclusions (though not involving breach of confidence) *Raja v Lloyd's TSB Bank*, [2000] Lloyd's Rep Bank 377 (mortgagee's duty to obtain a proper price); *Cia de Seguros Imperio v Heath (REBX) Ltd* [2001] 1 WLR 112 (CA) (breach of fiduciary duty); *Coulthard v Disco Mix Club Ltd* [2000] 1 WLR 707 (breach of fiduciary duty).

[41] Limitation Act 1980, s. 4A

Appendix A: Detriment

IS IT ESSENTIAL that the claimant in a confidentiality case should be able to show that the misuse of the information by the defendant was detrimental to her? Some judges have expressed the view (more or less tentatively) that it is.[1] Some that it is not.[2] Others that it is, but allowing 'detriment' so wide a meaning (in effect treating any misuse of confidential information as ipso facto detrimental), that it would not be required in any practical sense.[3] Others again have suggested that detriment is required in some cases (eg, government secrets) but not in others (eg, personal secrets).[4]

The restatement in this book takes the view that detriment *as such* is not in any sense a necessary requirement. But detriment in practice will often be relevant to the application of other principles. Thus: (*a*) whether publication would be expected to be detrimental is a relevant factor in assessing whether information is confidential at all (§ 2); (*b*) that publication or use would cause no harm to the claimant may lead the court to categorise the information as 'trivial', and therefore as unprotected (§ 8); (*c*) in applying the public interest limitation (§ 11) or deciding whether a prohibition on publication would unduly interfere with rights of freedom of expression (§ 17) detriment to the claimant (or its absence) is always important; (*d*) in deciding whether it would be inappropriate to grant an injunction because it would cause disproportionate hardship to the defendant to do so, the detriment to the claimant (or its absence) is relevant (§ 21), and will certainly be relevant in deciding whether an interim injunction should be granted (§ 22); (*e*) a court might refuse an account of profits where the

[1] See, eg, *Coco v A N Clark (Engineering) Ltd* [1969] RPC 41, 48 (Megarry J); *Attorney-General v Guardian Newspapers Ltd (No 2)* [1990] 1 AC 109, 270 (Lord Griffiths); *Douglas v Hello! Ltd (No 3)* [2005] EWCA Civ 595, [2006] QB 125, [118].

[2] *Federal Bank of the Middle East Ltd v Hadkinson* [2000] 2 All ER 395, 413 (Mummery LJ); *Smith Kline & French Laboratories (Australia) Ltd v Department of Community Services* [1990] FSR 617, 664 (Gummow J); *X v Y* [1988] 2 All ER 648, 657 (Rose J).

[3] Thus Lord Keith in *Attorney-General v Guardian Newspapers (No 2)*, [1990] 1 AC 109, 255–6: 'it is sufficient detriment to the confider that the information given in confidence is disclosed to persons he would prefer not to know of it'.

[4] Toulson & Phipps, para 3–165, so interpreting the requirement that publication be 'injurious to the public interest' stated by Lord Goff in relation to government secrets in *Attorney-General v Guardian Newspapers Ltd (No 2)* [1990] 1 AC 109, 283.

claimant had suffered no detriment and the defendant had acted in good faith (§ 23); (*f*) no damages will be awarded unless the claimant has suffered some quantifiable loss (§ 24).

When one puts all those instances together, it is easy to see that a claimant who has suffered (or would be expected to suffer) no adverse effect from the publication or use of information is very unlikely to succeed in obtaining any remedy. In practical terms, detriment is likely to matter, therefore. But by the same token it is quite unnecessary to add it as an *independent* and free-standing requirement for liability. A defendant who breaches a duty of confidence is not held liable because he has harmed the claimant by breaching confidence, but simply because he has breached confidence. It is better to understand it as a factor reflected, in various different ways, in the application of other more specific rules.

Appendix B: Information and Property

INFORMATION IS NOT PROPERTY

IT IS NOW clear that, in English law, information is not property. That is to say, English law does not impose duties upon people with respect to confidential information because it recognises some particular relationship between the claimant and the information (a right, as it were, *in rem*) which requires protection against strangers. Rather, it imposes duties between individuals (rights *in personam*) whose consequence is to protect information. Despite occasional wobbles or confusions,[1] this has been a fairly consistent theme: the equitable duty of confidence is not equivalent to a right *in rem* or *erga omnes*—but is a right which exists between people. The point was made early in the development of the principles, in *Morison v Moat*,[2] in which Turner V-C said that what he had to consider was 'not the right of the plaintiffs against the world, but their right against the defendant'. More than a hundred years later, the principle was lucidly restated by Lord Upjohn in *Boardman v Phipps*:

> the real truth is that [information] is not property in the normal sense but equity will restrain its transmission to another if in breach of some confidential relationship.[3]

It was most recently re-stated by the Court of Appeal and the House of Lords in *Douglas v Hello! Ltd (No 3)*.[4]

The protection of information thus depends on the existence of personal duties, and in that sense information is not property. The 'rational basis' of the law of confidence does not 'lie in proprietary right'.[5] That proposition,

[1] Such as Lord Hodson's comments in *Boardman v Phipps* [1967] 2 AC 46 (HL), 107. It is also likely that, in its *origins*, the protection of confidentiality was closely related to intellectual property rights: see D J Ibbetson, *A Historical Introduction to the Law of Obligations* (Oxford, 1999) 187.

[2] (1851) 9 Hare 241, 255.

[3] [1967] 2 AC 46 (HL), 127.

[4] [2005] EWCA Civ 595, [2006] QB 125, [119], reversed but approved on this point [2007] UKHL 21, [2007] 2 WLR 920, especially at [275] (Lord Walker).

[5] *Moorgate Tobacco Co Ltd v Philip Morris Ltd (No 2)* (1984) 156 CLR 414, 438 (Deane J). See also the useful discussion by the Supreme Court of Canada in *Cadbury Schweppes Inc v FBI Foods Ltd* [2000] FSR 491.

however, turns out to be almost completely useless as a way of arriving at any practical conclusions, and there are all sorts of ways in which it may be perfectly helpful to think of information *as if* it were a sort of property.

(*a*) Information is valuable. It can be valuable to have, and doubly valuable to have on an exclusive basis. So confidential information, if properly protected by law, is even more valuable, and the protection offered by the law increases its value. Information can in this sense be 'sold' (ie, transmitted to someone for money), and by an appropriately structured transaction may be sold on an exclusive basis (ie, transmitted in a way that gives the purchaser the benefit of exclusivity). Information, even if not property, is certainly capable of being the object of commercial transactions, and appropriately regarded in commercial terms as an 'asset'. The protection offered by the law of confidentiality helps to establish and maintain the value of such assets; it does not follow that they are property rights in the legal sense, any more than assets such as goodwill are property rights.

(*b*) Rights in respect of information may be property. A contractual right to use information, if assignable, or to prevent others from using or disclosing information, if assignable, is a species of intangible property. The same could be true of equitable rights.[6] The mechanism of assignment potentially converts any assignable personal right into a form, albeit a rather special form, of intangible property.

(*c*) It is often natural to use property language in relation to information, in a metaphorical sense. Thus, for instance, one can speak of the 'owner' of information, such as a trade secret. One can say it is *their* information. This is really simply a form of shorthand. Everyone understands that these expressions mean something along the lines of:

> a person who has a reasonable expectation of confidentiality in relation to this information and to whom duties of confidence are owed by others who are privy to the information which enables that person to control the way the information is used or disseminated.

In other words, we use 'owner' to indicate a person to whom others owe duties of confidence. This is a reflection of the undoubted fact that, given a reasonably rigorous set of rules protecting confidential information, it becomes protected *as if* it were, in many respects, a form of property. Property language is used as a convenient short-hand to avoid cumbersome statements of complex legal relationships between persons.

(*d*) In a similar vein, property language may be used to describe more complex situations. Thus one may say that information is trust property,[7] or partnership property.[8] Here again, however, property language is being used as a convenient

[6] See p __ above.

[7] *Green v Folgham* (1823) 1 Sim & St 398, 406, Leach V-C ('a trustee of this secret').

[8] *Dean v MacDowell* (1878) 8 Ch D 345 (CA), 354 (Cotton LJ); *Aas v Benham* [1891] 2 Ch 244 (CA), 258 (Bowen LJ).

shorthand to express rights between persons: the right of the beneficiaries to the income derived from exploitation of information by the trustee, or of partners to share in the income derived from exploitation of the secret. Rather as it is sometimes convenient to speak of partnerships or unincorporated associations *as if* they were legal persons, when they are not, so it is sometimes convenient to speak of information as if it were property, when it is not.

PROPRIETARY REMEDIES FOR BREACH OF CONFIDENCE

Somewhat related to the question whether information is property is the question whether, apart from the personal remedies of injunction, damages and account of profits, the claimant whose information is misused may claim a property interest in the 'fruits' of the defendant's misuse. For instance, if *A* gives confidential information to *B*, and *B* wrongfully writes a book that contains the confidential information, *A* is obviously entitled to an account of the profits *B* makes from the book. But can *A* also claim to be the equitable owner of the copyright, which *B* would then hold for *A* as constructive trustee? This question may be approached from a number of angles: on the basis of authority; from the perspective of a theory that explains when constructive trusts are to be imposed; and from a practical point of view.

Authority. In *Spycatcher* some of the judges thought that the answer was probably, Yes.[9] They thought it arguable that Peter Wright held the copyright of *Spycatcher* (the book he had written using confidential information) on constructive trust for the Crown. In two subsequent English decisions, however, a court has declined to treat property acquired (or whose acquisition was contributed to) by a breach of confidence as subject to a constructive trust.[10] To make the position still more muddled, there is yet a further decision in which the Court of Appeal seems to have accepted that breach of confidence might give rise to a constructive trust.[11] But it is complicated by the facts (*a*) that the Court of Appeal seemed to have in mind some sort of *remedial* constructive trust, which is in itself unorthodox,[12] and (*b*) that the case involved not just the misuse of confidential information, but its misuse by a fiduciary, which might form an independent basis for such a trust, and seems to have been at the forefront of the court's approach.

Theoretical considerations. Taking the theoretical perspective, one may ask whether (as a general matter) the imposition of a constructive trust over the

[9] [1990] 1 AC 109 (CA and HL), 211 (Dillon LJ), 263 (Lord Keith), 275–6 (Lord Griffiths), 288 (Lord Goff).

[10] *Satnam Investments Ltd v Dunlop Heywood & Co Ltd* [1999] 3 All ER 652 (CA); *Ocular Sciences Ltd v Aspect Vision Care Ltd* [1997] RPC 289.

[11] *United Pan-Europe Communications NV v Deutsche Bank AG* [2000] 2 BCLC 461 (CA).

[12] [2000] BCLC 461, [43] (Morritt LJ) 'leaving the court to determine *in the exercise of its discretion* what *remedy* to *impose*' (emphasis added).

'product' of a breach of confidence forms a coherent development of the circumstances in which a constructive trust is generally imposed. That inquiry is somewhat embarrassed by the fact that there is no current agreement about exactly what those circumstances are. But one may canvass three possibilities. First, it might be that constructive trusts exist where *fiduciaries* profit from their fiduciary position. That is probably too wide a statement. But even if it were correct, it would not follow that a constructive trust would be imposed in by any means every (or even most) breach of confidence cases. A duty of confidence is an equitable duty; it may arise out of a fiduciary relationship; but it is not itself a fiduciary duty. Secondly, it could be that constructive trust remedies are imposed where a person receives property for which she is *immediately accountable* to a third person.[13] Again, if that is correct, one would not expect constructive trusts to be a standard feature of breach of confidence claims. The person who breaches confidence is not immediately accountable for any profit. Whether or not she must account depends on whether the court (as a matter of discretion) orders an account. And if an account is ordered, it will be of the *profits*, not the proceeds or product, of the breach. Thirdly, it could be argued that a constructive trust depends on the product being the traceable proceeds of some *property* which the defendant originally held as a fiduciary for another.[14] If so, confidentiality is not fertile ground for proprietary constructive trusts, since (as was explained above) information is *not* generally regarded as property. In using confidential information to produce some item of property, the defendant does not convert one form of property into another; there is therefore no specifically proprietary justification for treating the product as owned by the person to whom the duty of confidence was owed.

Thus, on any one of the plausible theoretical views of the circumstances in which it is appropriate to regard the defendant as holding property acquired by wrongdoing on a (true) constructive trust for another, the product of confidential information seems unlikely to be so held—or, at least, if it is so held it will be because of something about the relationship of claimant and defendant other than the mere fact that the information is confidential.

Practical considerations. Looking to the practical side, one may ask whether it is practically or pragmatically desirable that a proprietary remedy should be made available. In this context, one has to bear four things in mind. (*a*) A proprietary 'remedy' is not truly a remedy at all, but a right which precedes and is quite independent of any finding of liability. In English law, constructive trusts are not truly remedies but statements of property right. The court may *find* that property is held on constructive trust; but where it does so its view of the legal position is given retrospective effect. Moreover, it is not a matter of discretion. The court cannot choose whether or not to impose a constructive trust on

[13] G Virgo, *Principles of the Law of Restitution*, 2nd edn (Oxford, 2006) 529.

[14] P Millett, 'Proprietary Restitution' in S Degeling and J Edelman (eds), *Equity in Commercial Law* (Pyrmont, 2005) ch 12.

discretionary grounds.[15] (*b*) Where property is held on constructive trust, that trust affects third parties who obtain the property in question subject only to a defence of *bona fide* purchase. If, for instance, property held on constructive trust is given by D_1 (a wrongdoer) to D_2 (a volunteer), then D_2 holds that property on constructive trust. Or if the property is given by D_1 (a wrongdoer) to D_2 (a purchaser), the equitable doctrine of constructive notice applies with its full rigour. (*c*) The existence of a constructive trust over property in the hands of a defendant confers important advantages, in particular against an insolvent defendant, because it ensures that particular assets (those held on constructive trust) are ring-fenced for the enforcement of one claimant's claims, over and above those of other creditors. There is, however, a risk of unfairness to the defendant's general creditors if constructive trusts are extravagantly imposed. (*d*) It can in practical terms be difficult to establish how far any particular item of property has been acquired by a breach of confidence. Often its acquisition will be partly a consequence of a breach of confidence, but partly also the consequence of other innocent acts. In such circumstances, to treat the entire property as subject to a constructive trust might seem disproportionate, while to treat it as 'partly' subject to such a trust causes great difficulty and complexity.[16]

The proprietary constructive trust, therefore, is an institution which has far-reaching consequences for third parties (recipients of the trust property and creditors), in relation to which the court has no remedial discretion, and which often raises difficult questions of fact in identifying the trust property. These practical considerations, it is suggested, militate against treating property as subject to a constructive trust except in well-defined cases. There are clear and obvious reasons why, for instance, the person who dishonestly receives trust property should hold it on constructive trust. But it is not at all clear why, in the ordinary way at least, a person who commits the wrong of breach of confidence should do so. Consider two anomalies it would cause. Take first the wrongdoer herself. If a defendant breaches confidence, she *may* be required to account for her profits to the claimant. But she may not. The remedy might be withheld if it is disproportionate.[17] Why, then, should the defendant (who may not even be accountable for the amount of profits) hold the proceeds of a breach of confidence *in specie* on trust for the claimant? That conclusion, if valid, would undermine the whole discretionary remedial scheme.

Or take the third party recipient of information. If D_1 passes confidential information to D_2, who then uses it, D_2 will only be liable if she knew or had

[15] *Re Polly Peck International plc* (No 2) [1998] 3 All ER 812 (CA). Compare the apparent assumptions to the contrary in *United Pan-Europe Communications NV v Deutsche Bank AG* [2000] 2 BCLC 461, [43] (Morritt LJ), and of Laddie J in *Ocular Sciences Ltd v Aspect Vision Care Ltd* [1997] RPC 289, 416, both of which seemed to treat a constructive trust as some form of discretionary remedy.

[16] This seems to have been an important feature in the thinking of the Court of Appeal in *Satnam Investments Ltd v Dunlop Heywood & Co Ltd* [1999] 3 All ER 652, 663, and of Laddie J's views in *Ocular Sciences Ltd v Aspect Vision Care Ltd* [1997] RPC 289, 416.

[17] See above, pp 103 and 130.

notice of its confidentiality—and notice clearly does not mean constructive notice in the strict sense (it may, indeed, require actual knowledge).[18] Now suppose that instead of simply passing the information, D_1 writes it down and assigns the copyright in the written form of the information to D_2. If the comments in *Spycatcher* were correct, D_1 would hold the copyright on constructive trust for the claimant. It follows that D_2 would also hold the copyright on constructive trust for the claimant unless she could show that she was a bona fide purchaser for value without notice—using 'notice' this time in the strictest sense.[19] Thus, depending on whether D_2 used information to write a fresh work, or to use something D_1 happened to have written, significantly different liability principles might apply. This would be messy and unsatisfactory.

All would be quite different, of course, if English law recognised the *remedial* constructive trust. That would be a trust imposed *ex nunc*, with prospective rather than retrospective effect, at the time liability was determined. It would be discretionary. It would, accordingly, be flexible. It could avoid the practical problems identified above. The court could 'impose' a constructive trust over, for instance a 'complete discrete item of property' in a clear case, but withhold such a trust where it would be unreasonable or operate unfairly.[20] But, as things stand, it is not a possibility under English law. And it is by no means certain that it would be a desirable development, since it introduces what some might think to be a dangerous element of unpredictability into the grant of remedies.[21] So long as that position remains, it is suggested, the better view is that generally speaking an action for breach of confidence does not give rise to any sort of constructive trust.

This is not to say that there may not be cases where the product of a breach of confidence is held on constructive trust. But, it is suggested, such cases will always turn on the presence of some additional feature which makes a constructive trust appropriate, on conventional grounds, in the particular case.[22] Suppose, for instance, that *T* holds a trade secret on trust for *B*. If *T* wrongly licensed *X* to use that secret, and *X* knew that *T* was acting wrongfully, and then embodied the secret in, say, a set of plans, it might be appropriate to regard *X* as holding the copyright of the plans on constructive trust for *B*. The case would be very close to that in which *X* receives trust property of a conventional sort. It might justify the imposition of a constructive trust. But the trust would be imposed not simply because *X* was in breach of confidence, but principally

[18] See § 5.

[19] See *Attorney-General v Guardian Newspapers Ltd* (*No 2*) [1990] 1 AC 109, 139–40 (Scott J).

[20] *Ocular Sciences Ltd v Aspect Vision Care Ltd* [1997] RPC 289, 416 (Laddie J). The decision of the Supreme Court of Canada in *LAC Minerals Ltd v International Corona Resources Ltd* [1990] FSR 441, in which the constructive trust was clearly treated as a 'remedy': [1990] FSR 441, 469 (La Forest J). Laddie J seems inclined to treat it as such in *Ocular Sciences*; but with respect that approach is unorthodox.

[21] P Birks, 'The Remedies for Abuse of Confidential Information' [1990] *LMCLQ* 460.

[22] This could have provided a basis for such a trust in *United Pan-Europe Communications NV v Deutsche Bank AG* [2000] 2 BCLC 461 (CA).

because of *X*'s participation in a breach of the fiduciary duties that *T*, *as trustee*, owes *B*. The constructive trust, in such a case, does not arise as a result of any breach of confidence by *T* at all. Indeed, it is very likely that *T* owes *B* no duty of confidence as such; *T* is probably the beneficiary of duties of confidence with respect to the secret. The crucial duty owed by *T* to *B* is his duty, as trustee, to account to *B in specie* for the income generated by the exploitation of the secret. It is this duty (and *X*'s knowledge or notice of it) that provides a foundation for the constructive trust.

The view taken by the restatement here, therefore, is that as things stand there is no doctrine that a defendant holds the 'product' of a breach of confidence on constructive trust for the confidant. In particular circumstances (eg, where the breach of confidence is also a breach of trust or fiduciary duty), he may do. And there would be something to be said for a change in the law that permitted the court to impose, by its judgment and from the date of its judgment, a constructive trust over identifiable property in particular cases. But as things stand this is not an available option, and were it to be introduced it would be necessary to specify with some clarity how the discretion should be exercised.

Appendix C: Confidence and Privacy

THE CONCERNS

THE APPROACH TAKEN in this Restatement is that one set of common principles governs all types of claim that *D* owes *C* an obligation not to use or disclose information. A single cause of action (breach of confidence) protects a certain sort of right (the right to control the use by others of information), using one set of concepts, principles and remedies to do so. But there is a price to be paid for this unified approach. For it means that the same set of doctrines is put to work protecting a variety of different interests: the interests in personal autonomy and reputation we call 'privacy', commercial interests such as trade secrets, and the policy concerns underlying government secrecy. It also means that a single obligation derives from a number of varied moral claims—sometimes based on explicit consent; sometimes on the obligations which attach to consensual relationships; sometimes simply on the expectations and obligations necessary for civil society between strangers.

As a matter of positive law, for better or worse, this seems to be the position taken in English law.[1] Some have doubted whether it is sensible to suppose that a set of principles designed for one of these tasks can be appropriate to another. For instance, in *Douglas v Hello! Ltd (No 3)*, the Court of Appeal protested:

> We cannot pretend that we find it satisfactory to be required to shoehorn within the cause of action for breach of confidence claims for publication of unauthorized photographs of a private occasion.[2]

Echoing such concerns, the Court of Appeal of New Zealand declined to follow the English approach, preferring to develop separate torts of breach of

[1] The House of Lords has made it clear that English law does not contain a special 'privacy tort' (*Wainwright v Home Office* [2003] UKHL 53, [2004] 2 AC 406), and that issues of informational privacy are to be addressed by development of the action for breach of confidence (*Campbell v MGN Ltd* [2004] UKHL 22, [2004] 2 AC 457).

[2] [2005] EWCA Civ 595, [2006] QB 125, [53].

confidence and privacy.[3] Commentators too, from a variety of different perspectives, have doubted whether the unified approach is workable. These concerns deserve consideration. In order to address them it is necessary to tease out the principal grounds of scepticism.

THE PRIVATE AND THE CONFIDENTIAL

The first set of concerns relates to the distinction between the private and the confidential. From around the time the Human Rights Act 1998 was passed, human rights lawyers worried that the law of confidence tended to value and protect information only where it was in some way 'secret', and that this was likely to pose a problem in protecting private information because it was necessary to recognise a degree of privacy in public spaces. It was suggested that the first requirement recognised by Megarry J in *Coco v AN Clark (Engineers) Ltd*, namely that information must have the 'necessary quality of confidence about it'[4] was too narrow to protect privacy adequately. There was also concern that certain rather dated authorities—particularly *Woodward v Hutchins*[5]—might lead courts too readily to refuse protection to 'public acts', and that the doctrine that confidentiality is lost once information becomes publicly available might be used to similar effect.

These concerns do not appear to have been generally justified. There have been some questionable decisions, of course.[6] But it has become clear that, applying a test of 'reasonable expectation of privacy', the fact that something occurs in a place where it might be observed by the public does not prevent it from being protected.[7] Nor have courts accepted that public figures forego protection.[8] And the courts appear to be sensitive to the idea that information may be publicly available without ceasing to be protected.[9] The fact that not every decision seems perfect to every commentator hardly shows that the law's fundamental structure is at fault.

Such developments have allayed the concerns of human rights lawyers that the law of confidence cannot be used to provide a reasonably adequate framework

[3] *Hosking v Runting* [2005] 1 NZLR 1.

[4] [1969] RPC 41, 47 (Megarry J).

[5] [1977] 1 WLR 760 (CA).

[6] Particularly *Theakston v MGN Ltd* [2002] EMLR 22, which has been heavily criticised. See, eg, G Phillipson, 'Transforming Breach of Confidence? Towards a Common Law Right of Privacy under the Human Rights Act' (2003) 66 *MLR* 726, 737. See also A McLean and C Mackey, 'Is There a Law of Privacy in the UK? A Consideration of Recent Legal Developments' (2007) 29 *EIPR* 389, 390–1, criticising *John v Associated Newspapers Ltd* [2006] EWHC 1611 (QB), [2006] EMLR 27, in which Eady J refused to enjoin publication of a photograph, taken in a public street, of Elton John which showed his baldness.

[7] See p 10 above.

[8] See p 94 above.

[9] See p 38 above.

for the protection of some privacy rights.[10] However, they have simultaneously concerned intellectual property lawyers, worried that they involve 'impermissible violence to the principles on which the cause of action is founded'.[11] In particular, it has been suggested that the shift from a test based on the 'necessary quality of confidence' to one based on 'reasonable expectations of privacy', and what is said to be relaxation of the requirement that information be secret and not publicly available if it is to be confidential, risks unduly extending protection in commercial cases.[12]

It is suggested that the critics somewhat overstate their case, in two respects. First, they exaggerate the clarity and the rigidity of the 'traditional' law. Many examples could be given, but two will suffice. Consider the 'traditional' test, that information should have the 'necessary quality of confidence'. That has been held up as an example of a clear standard now under threat.[13] But what did it actually mean? It seems doubtful that the newer test ('reasonable expectation of confidentiality or privacy') is any vaguer or less workable than a search for some elusive 'quality of confidence'. Or consider the suggestion that the 'traditional law' contained a 'fairly stringent'[14] requirement that information be 'secret or inaccessible' to the public[15], which has now been laid aside. The truth is more complex. There was certainly never a rule that publicly observable information could not be confidential.[16] So, too, how far information could enter the public domain and yet remain confidential was long recognised as a question of fact and degree.[17] So it remains.

Secondly, even as it has developed, the fact that the law applies the same basic principles in commercial and non-commercial cases does not mean that it must reach the same result. Context matters, and the context includes the type of information and the reasons why it is protected. In *Campbell*[18] the House of Lords found that privacy attached to a photograph of a *person* taken in sensitive circumstances on a public street. It does not follow that a manufacturer who drove a prototype car on quiet public roads would have any expectation of confidentiality.[19] It is vital to understand that just because the law does not

[10] Of course 'privacy' is not limited to control over the use or disclosure of personal information. It covers other, distinct interests, such as the protection of personal space or the home, and family relationships. See R Mulheron, 'A Potential Framework for Privacy? A Reply to Hello' (2006) 69 *MLR* 679, 696–8. It seems unrealistic to suppose that all these interests should be protected by one tort.

[11] Bingham, 'Should There Be a Law to Protect Rights of Personal Privacy' [1996] EHRLR 450, 457.

[12] See, eg, T Aplin, 'Commercial Confidences After the Human Rights Act' (2007) 29 *EIPR* 411, 411–14.

[13] Aplin, *ibid*, 411; Mulheron, n 10 above, 687 describes it as 'grossly affected' by recent developments.

[14] Aplin, n 12 above, 413.

[15] Aplin, n 12 above, 412.

[16] See, eg, *Exchange Telegraph Co Ltd v Central News Ltd* [1897] 2 Ch 48.

[17] See, eg, *Schering Chemicals Ltd v Falkman* [1982] QB 1 (CA), 28 (Shaw LJ), 37 (Templeman LJ).

[18] [2004] UKHL 22, [2004] 2 AC 457.

[19] To take the example given by Aplin, n 12 above, 412, citing A Sims, '"A Shift in the Centre of Gravity": The Dangers of Protecting Privacy through Breach of Confidence' [2005] IPQ 27.

construct quite different rules for different types of information, it is not committed to disregarding relevant differences. In a variety of ways the approach will be tailored to the particular case—for instance in deciding whether information is confidential at all, or whether confidentiality has been lost by publication, or what weight should be attached to confidentiality in assessing whether it outweighs any right to freedom of expression.

There can be no doubt that absorbing modern concerns with privacy has required some development of the law of confidence. It seems doubtful, however, whether it should fairly be characterised as 'impermissible violence'. The developments have not involved fundamental change, but rather somewhat increased flexibility in areas where there was already a fairly high degree of flexibility. The law remains alert to the particular context of each case, and the need to treat different kinds of information with appropriate sensitivity to context.

THE REDUCED SIGNIFICANCE OF RELATIONSHIPS

A second, different, development about which sceptics worry is the removal of the imperative need for any confidential relationship as the foundation for a duty of confidence. There is no doubt that any such requirement, such as stated by Megarry J in *Coco v Clark*,[20] has been 'firmly shaken off'.[21] This seems, to some, a matter of regret,[22] effecting a fundamental change in the law.

This seems questionable. Long before the Human Rights Act, the action for breach of confidence had been treated as applicable in cases where no pre-existing confidential relationship could be found: to information acquired by chance or accident,[23] the fruits of industrial espionage,[24] intrusive surveillance,[25] or mistake.[26] Megarry J's second requirement, therefore, was looking pretty threadbare—and in cases which had nothing to do with 'privacy'—long before the Human Rights Act 1998. Cases such as these could not be explained as cases where 'trust had been abused':[27] the claimant had reposed no trust in the defendant, even in some extended sense. Moreover, as with the distinction between personal privacy and commercial confidentiality, the fact that it is unnecessary always to establish a relationship of 'trust and confidence' does not mean that the law is blind to the existence of such a relationship, or its absence.

[20] [1969] RPC 41, 47.

[21] *Campbell v MGN Ltd* [2004] UKHL 22, [2004] 2 AC 457, [14] (Lord Nicholls).

[22] *Hosking v Runting* [2005] 1 NZLR 1, [49] (Gault P); *Campbell v MGN Ltd* [2002] EWCA Civ 1373, [2003] QB 633, [70] (Lord Phillips MR); Aplin, n 12 above, 415 (describing it as 'regrettable' that the requirement should not apply to commercial information).

[23] The 'confidential document . . . wafted out of a window': *Attorney-General v Guardian Newspapers (No 2)* [1990] 1 AC 109 (HL), 281 (Lord Goff).

[24] *Franklin v Giddins* [1978] Qd R 72.

[25] *Hellewell v Chief Constable of Derbyshire* [1995] 1 WLR 804, 807 (Laws J).

[26] *English & American Insurance Co v Herbert Smith* [1988] FSR 232.

[27] *Douglas v Hello! Ltd* [2001] QB 967, 1011 (Sedley LJ) (drawing a distinction between confidentiality, the protection against abuse of trust, and privacy, unwanted intrusion).

It does not make the identification of such relationships a *sine qua non* of liability, or regard the sole purpose of the law as their enforcement. But that is not a new development, but the continuation of a line of thought clearly present even in 'traditional' cases. And the law remains thoroughly alert to their significance.

ADVANTAGES OF THE CURRENT APPROACH

For the reasons given above, it is suggested that complaints that 'impermissible violence' has been done to the 'traditional' law of confidentiality have been overstated. But is there any positive advantage to the current position?

If English law decided to divide 'confidentiality' law from 'privacy' law, and address each using distinctly different rules, it would be necessary to identify the dividing line. It is not clear where critics feel that line would be drawn. One possibility is that it might lie along the boundary between 'commercial' secrets and 'personal' privacy, that is along a line which represents distinct *interests*.[28] That, however, is not always a clear line. Were *Douglas v Hello! Ltd*[29] or *Browne v Associated Newspapers*[30] cases of personal privacy, or commercial confidentiality? They had elements of both. Nor is it in any sense a traditional line. It is plain that, from its earliest days, the law of confidence—understood in its most traditional and orthodox way—has been called upon to protect 'personal' privacy[31] and that its animating values have always included the protection of personal privacy interests. To carve these cases out of the law of confidence, on the ground that 'personal privacy' is to be protected by its own separate tort on different principles from commercial confidences, would itself be a novel development. As things stand, it is arguably a merit of the law that it can accommodate what is relevantly distinctive about such cases without requiring precise boundaries to be drawn.

An alternative approach would be to draw the line based on the presence or absence of a relationship of trust and confidence, that is on the rationale underlying the obligations imposed by law. Where the rationale is essentially consensual, the traditional rules would be applied. Where it is not, the new law of privacy would apply. The difficulty with that approach, however, is that it makes it hard to accommodate—except as gross anomalies—those cases which the traditional law recognises as instances of confidence quite apart from relationship,[32] at least some of which it would be hard to regard as cases of privacy. Moreover, here too the lines are perhaps not as clear as they appear. Between the close voluntary confidant and the complete stranger who happens to

[28] See, eg, Aplin n 12 above.

[29] [2007] UKHL 21, [2007] 2 WLR 920.

[30] [2007] EWCA Civ 296, [2007] 3 WLR 289.

[31] *Prince Albert v Strange* (1849) 1 Mac & G 25; *Pollard v Photographic Co* (1888) 40 Ch D 345; *Argyll v Argyll* [1967] Ch 302.

[32] See nn 23–6 above.

discover some fact there is not so much a clear line as a spectrum of more-or-less close relationships.

Although it is often (and fairly) asserted that privacy and confidentiality are different concepts,[33] embodying different values,[34] they have a family resemblance, and often co-exist in individual cases. The archetypal case of pure confidentiality is, perhaps, the case of the contractual obligation to keep some confidential secret. The archetypal case of the pure privacy interest is the case of the stranger who happens to observe or record some intimate moment. But between these two extremes are many cases which blend elements of both archetypes, and in which the values of both are in play. If lovers kiss and tell, for instance, their disclosure implicates both personal autonomy and trust; it will have personal and reputational consequences, but it may also have commercial and economic consequences. And there are common features even of cases at opposite extremes. At least *some* element of limited knowledge seems to be relevant to privacy, for instance, as it is to confidentiality. The porn star who *decides* to share his intimate moments with the paying public is hardly entitled to protection, however fundamental sexuality may be to personal autonomy.

There is no perfect response to such complexity; there are several different lines that might be drawn. The English response, which is to adopt a single set of principles but apply them with some sensitivity to context is, it is suggested, a defensible one. Alternatives, which would attempt to create specialised bodies of rules to address different situations, would not necessarily produce a more satisfactory overall result.

[33] *Hosking v Runting* [2005] 1 NZLR 1, [48] (Gault P); Mulheron, n 10 above, 692–4.
[34] Phillipson, n 6 above, 728.

Index

www.ingramcontent.com/pod-product-compliance
Lightning Source LLC
LaVergne TN
LVHW011803200926
848484LV00003B/771